THE ULTIMATE
Preschool Activity Guide

Over 200 fun preschool learning activities for ages 3-5

Autumn McKay

Find me on Instagram!
@BestMomIdeas

The Ultimate Preschool Activity Guide by Autumn McKay
Published by Creative Ideas Publishing

www.BestMomIdeas.com

For permissions contact:
Permissions@BestMomIdeas.com

ISBN: 978-1-952016-37-0

Table of Contents

About Me...xi

Introduction xii

All About Me Activities 1

LOW PREP All About Me Book.. 2

LOW PREP Draw Yourself with Chalk.................................. 3

LOW PREP Measure Body Parts.. 4

Name Collage 5

Playdough Feelings Faces.. 6

Apples 7

ABC Apple Matching 8

Apple Names 8

Apple Picking 9

LOW PREP Apple Printing...10

LOW PREP Apple Seed Counting 10

LOW PREP Apple Taste Test 11

LOW PREP Parts of an Apple 11

Around the World 12

Africa

LOW PREP Passport...13

LOW PREP African Collar Necklace....................................14

Animal Puzzles..15

LOW PREP Build the Nile River 16

Shisima 17

Antarctica

LOW PREP Passport...18

LOW PREP Blubber Experiment 19

LOW PREP Snowball Counting 20

Snowflake Building 21

Why do Ice Cubes Melt? 21

Table of Contents

Asia

`LOW PREP` Passport 22

`LOW PREP` Chinese Writing Tray 23

`LOW PREP` Chopstick Transfer 24

`LOW PREP` Japanese Carp Kites 25

`LOW PREP` Make a Chinese Lantern 26

Australia

`LOW PREP` Passport 27

`LOW PREP` Aboriginal Boomerang 28

`LOW PREP` Build a Koala 28

Damper Bread 29

Kangaroo Name 30

Europe

`LOW PREP` Passport 31

`LOW PREP` German Transportation 32

`LOW PREP` Pouring Tea 32

`LOW PREP` Reloj 33

Spaghetti Painting 34

North America

`LOW PREP` Passport 35

Maple Syrup Playdough 36

`LOW PREP` North America Maze 37

`LOW PREP` Pull Open Pinata 38

`LOW PREP` Scrap Paper Sombreros 39

South America

`LOW PREP` Passport 40

`LOW PREP` Country Syllable Count 41

`LOW PREP` Living vs. Nonliving in South America 42

Paper Chain Snake Patterns 43

Zamponas 44

Table of Contents

Bees...45

   Add and Subtract Bees..46

   LOW PREP Bee Life Cycle..47

   LOW PREP Bee Mask..48

   LOW PREP Bee Pollen Counting.....................................48

   LOW PREP Bumblebee Number Line................................49

   LOW PREP Flying Bee Cutting..50

   LOW PREP Label Parts of a Bee.....................................51

   Nectar Relay..52

   Paper Bag Bumblebee...53

   LOW PREP Stripe Counting...54

Bears..55

   Bear Hunt Sequence...56

   LOW PREP Bear Patterns...57

   Bear Paw Names...58

   Feed the Bear..59

   LOW PREP Gummy Bear Science....................................60

   LOW PREP Make a Bear Cave..61

   LOW PREP Teddy Bear More or Less...............................61

Birds...62

   Bird Sorting..63

   LOW PREP Birdseed Writing..63

   LOW PREP Feather Cutting...64

   LOW PREP Feather Painting..64

   Paper Plate Birds..65

   LOW PREP Parts of a Bird...66

Body Systems...67

  Circulatory

   LOW PREP Beat the Clock..68

   Blood Bottle...69

   LOW PREP Circulatory Coloring.....................................70

Table of Contents

LOW PREP Heart Pump..71

LOW PREP Measure Heart Beat..72

Digestive

LOW PREP Digest Food Experiment..73

LOW PREP Digestive Tract Sequencing...74

LOW PREP How Long are the Small Intestines?..........................75

LOW PREP Taste Buds Collage..76

Muscles

LOW PREP Make it Stronger..76

LOW PREP Muscle Model...77

Obstacle Course...78

Nervous

LOW PREP Amazing Brain..79

Brain Hat...80

Memory Game...81

Spine Model..82

Skeleton

Bone Letters..83

LOW PREP Make a Skeleton..84

LOW PREP Why are Bones Important?..85

Pancakes vs. Cookie...86

Respiratory

Lung Craft...87

LOW PREP Lung Race...87

LOW PREP Measure Lung Capacity...88

LOW PREP Paper Bag Lungs..89

Butterflies..90

Butterfly Addition..91

Caterpillar Patterns...92

Coffee Filter Butterfly..93

LOW PREP How to Draw a Butterfly..94

LOW PREP Noodle Life Cycle..95

Pollen Transfer..96

LOW PREP Very Hungry Caterpillar Sequence.............................97

Table of Contents

Construction 98

LOW PREP Add Nuts and Bolts...99

LOW PREP Build Letters with Rocks.................................100

LOW PREP Count and Wreck...101

LOW PREP Hammer Syllables...102

Measuring...103

LOW PREP Play with Nuts, Bolts, and Washers 103

LOW PREP Sort Pom Poms...104

LOW PREP What Can You Create?...104

Cooking 105

Applesauce...106

LOW PREP Banana Split Pudding Cups...107

Chocolate Bark...108

LOW PREP Pizza...109

LOW PREP Popcorn on the Cob...110

LOW PREP Rainbow Milk Toast 111

LOW PREP Sausage Balls...112

LOW PREP Sensory Measuring...113

LOW PREP Smoothie...113

Sprinkle Counting...114

Dinosaurs 115

Build a Dinosaur...116

LOW PREP Catch the Dinosaur...116

Dinosaur Fossils...117

Dinosaur Name...118

LOW PREP Dinosaur Puppets...119

Dinosaur Sort...120

Rescue the Dinosaurs 121

Engineer...122

LOW PREP House Building...123

LOW PREP Magic Stars...124

LOW PREP Make a Bouncy Ball...125

LOW PREP Make a Harmonica...126

LOW PREP Playdough Marble Race Track...127

Table of Contents

LOW PREP Which Shape is Strongest? 128

Family 129

Dotted Family Names 130

Family Match 131

Family Scavenger Hunt 132

LOW PREP Tube Family 133

LOW PREP Who Lives in Your House? 134

Friendship 135

LOW PREP Being a Friend Sort 136

LOW PREP Cotton Ball vs. Sandpaper Words 137

LOW PREP Fill the Bucket 138

LOW PREP Friendship Bracelet 139

LOW PREP Hands are Not for Hitting 140

LOW PREP Pass the Ice Cream 140

Gardening 141

LOW PREP Explore Seeds 142

Flower Counting 142

LOW PREP Leaf Stamping 143

LOW PREP Plant Seeds 144

LOW PREP Seed Names 144

Sort Seeds 145

Healthy Habits 146

LOW PREP Blow Paint Germ Hands 147

Brush Away Letters 147

Egg Brushing Experiment 148

LOW PREP Fruit and Vegetable Patterns 149

LOW PREP Germ Washing Station 150

LOW PREP Healthy Food Beginning Sounds 150

LOW PREP Healthy vs. Unhealthy Sort 151

LOW PREP Inside and Outside Food Match 151

LOW PREP Toothbrush Writing 152

LOW PREP Workout Rotation 153

Table of Contents

Money...154

  LOW PREP Clean Coins...155

  LOW PREP Coin Boats..156

  LOW PREP Coin Counting 157

  Coin Deposit Bank...157

  Coin Eggs...158

  Coin Letters...158

  LOW PREP Coin Matching..159

  LOW PREP Coin Sorting..159

  LOW PREP Coin Stack...160

  LOW PREP Don't Break the Bank.................................160

Opposites...161

  Foot Trail...162

  LOW PREP Opposites Board Game..............................163

  LOW PREP Opposites Coloring.....................................163

  LOW PREP Opposite Day..164

  LOW PREP Simon Says Opposites................................164

Simple Machines.. 165

  Inclined Plane Art...166

  Launching Balls...167

  LOW PREP Playground Pulley.......................................168

  LOW PREP Wedge Experiment.....................................169

  Wheel and Axel Car..170

Scissor Skills 171

  LOW PREP Cut Gummy Worms 172

  LOW PREP Cut Junk Mail..172

  LOW PREP Cut Paint Samples......................................173

  LOW PREP Cut Playdough..173

  Cut and Rescue...174

  Cut Spaghetti..174

  LOW PREP Cut Straws...175

Table of Contents

Sports..176

  LOW PREP Baseball Prewriting.................................177

Basketball Counting..177

Football Letter Matching...178

Mini Ice Hockey..179

Paper Plate Skating...179

Soccer Ball Math...180

Spy Training..181

  LOW PREP Fingerprint Science...............................182

  LOW PREP Invisible Ink Message...........................183

Laser Beam Obstacle...183

  LOW PREP Secret Code Message...........................184

  LOW PREP What's Missing?...................................184

Water..185

Frozen Paintbrushes..186

  LOW PREP Keep Paper Dry Experiment.................187

  LOW PREP Leak-Proof Bag...................................188

Monster Battle...188

  LOW PREP Oil and Water.....................................189

  LOW PREP Walking Water....................................190

  LOW PREP Water Absorption................................191

  LOW PREP What Dissolves in Water.......................191

Appendix...193

About Me

My name is Autumn. I am a wife to an incredible husband, and a mother to two precious boys and a sweet little girl! My children are currently seven, five, and three years old.

I have a Bachelor's of Science degree in Early Childhood Education. I have taught in the classroom and as an online teacher. I have earned teacher certifications in Arizona, Colorado, California, and Georgia. However, one of my greatest joys is being a mom! After my first son was born, I wanted to be involved in helping him learn and grow so I began to develop color lessons to help engage his developing mind. I also wanted to help other moms dealing with hectic schedules and continuous time restraints. These activities evolved into my first book, called *Toddler Lesson Plans: Learning Colors*.

All of my children and I have had the pleasure of doing activities together. They each have a love of learning, so much so, I wanted to share the new activities with you and your children. The book you hold in your hands, **The Ultimate Preschool Activity Guide**, is full of activities I know your preschooler will enjoy too. These activities are focused around a theme, and provide a fun and educational experience for you and your preschooler. Through my learning time with my children, I have created the following books:

Toddler Lesson Plans: Learning ABC's

The Ultimate Toddler Activity Guide

The Ultimate Kindergarten Prep Guide

Learning Numbers Workbook

Learning Preschool Math Workbook

Learning Kindergarten Math Workbook

Learning 1st Grade Math Workbook

Learning ABC's Workbook: Print

Learning ABC's Workbook: Precursive

I hope that your little ones can benefit from these activities just like my children! I have also developed a website called **BestMomIdeas.com**. It's a place where moms are encouraged to be the best version of themselves by feeling understood and never judged.

Introduction

Benefits of Activity Time

Did you know that 90% of a child's brain develops by age 5? This means that almost all of a child's brain is developed before they reach kindergarten! So, take advantage of your preschooler's brain development in the early years by beginning or continuing an activity time!

"Activity time" refers to activating or stimulating a child's body and/or brain. This typically involves a hands-on experience for the preschooler where he is engaged in reading, running, climbing, coloring, pouring, etc.

Let me explain how the brain develops. When a baby is born, he is born with all the neurons (brain cells) that he will have for the rest of his life. Although most of the brain's neurons are present at birth, the neurons are not mature. Neurons have branches called dendrites and axons that transfer information from neuron to neuron. These branches on the neurons are crucial in brain development. The number of branches increases dramatically as a child is exposed to things around him. If the connections are used regularly, then they stay. But if the connections aren't used, they are pruned and die off. The more stimulation or exposure to experiences a child has, the thicker the connections become. It's much harder for these connections to be formed later in life.

Loving interactions with parents or caregivers help prepare a brain for learning. Every time you play, read, cook, garden, color, or do an educational activity with your child, these activities are building connections in your child's developing brain.

Additional Helpful Hints

This book includes activities from many different topics that preschoolers are naturally curious about such as the human body, bears, machines, sports and many more. I recommend reading through the table of contents to find a theme that interests your preschooler. Once you find a theme your preschooler will enjoy, you can turn to the corresponding page to find a materials list and step by step instructions for each activity. Each activity should only take 10 to 20 minutes because we all know that a preschooler's attention span is very short.

For each activity, I suggest that you ask your preschooler if he wants to do a fun activity instead of making him do it, so that the learning experience is enjoyable. Some days, my children will tell me that they do not want to do an activity, and that is totally fine! However, most days my children will ask when it is activity time. It makes this mommy's heart happy knowing that they want to learn!

I know many parents are very busy and do not have a lot of time to set up an activity so I have placed a "low prep" ribbon beside all activities that should only take a minute or two to prep. I hope these low/no prep activities make life just a little easier for you, especially on busy days.

To help you prepare your materials in advance, look ahead at the next set of activities you want to do with your preschooler. At this time, make a list of all the materials you will need to buy during your next shopping trip to the grocery store. To help make life a little easier for you, you can access a comprehensive materials list for each activity theme through the link in "A Gift for You."

A Gift for You

In appreciation of your purchase of this book, I would like to provide a link to the printable appendix pages. This will allow you to have access to appendix pages in color so you can do your preschooler's favorite activity again and again.

www.bestmomideas.com/ultimate-preschool-printouts

Password: bestmomideas9mx4

Play Your Way to Learning

Nothing is more charming than a child's face and the many expressions of joy a child exhibits in play and learning. Learning can be so fun! Playtime can be an enjoyable moment for the entire family. Throughout these pages, you will find many wonderful activities which hold the potential to bring a smile to your child's face and joy in your home. My hope is that in the midst of your children "playing their way" to growth and knowledge, this book will help flood your home with joy.

As you begin your journey through this book, I need to mention that in most of the activities, I address your child with the pronoun "he." I did this for simplicity and ease of writing; however, please know, as I wrote this book I was thinking of your precious little girl as well. I also want to reiterate that the goal of this book is to provide activities that you can enjoy with your child. The activities in this book are written for the preschooler. However, these years are a time of many developmental milestones. Each child is unique and matures at his or her own pace. If you sense your preschooler is becoming frustrated with an activity, please be sensitive and do not push your child to continue. Without question, you know your child best and what he is capable of attempting. If you feel an activity is beyond your child's present ability, simply move to another activity. There are many great "child tested" activities from which to choose.

Remember, even though significant learning will occur as you engage your child in these activities, I want you and your child to have fun! Often when my children pray, they each end their prayer with the statement, "...And let us have a fun day, Amen." In the midst of hectic days and the constant pressure to perform, a child deserves a fun day. The truth is you deserve a "fun day" as well. It is my desire that in the following pages you will discover a path for your preschooler to learn, and an avenue through which you will experience immense satisfaction as YOU have a fun day and enjoy your child.

I hope these activities bring as much joy and learning to your home as they have mine!

Activities

All About Me

LOW PREP *All About Me Book*

Materials:

- ☐ All About Me Book Activity Pages (Appendix A)
- ☐ Crayons
- ☐ Construction Paper
- ☐ Scissors
- ☐ Stapler

Directions:

There are two book pages on each sheet of the *All About Me Book* activity pages, so you will need to cut the pages in half to assemble the book.

1. Ask your preschooler if he would enjoy making a book that is all about him!

2. Let your preschooler pick his favorite color of construction paper.

3. Fold the construction paper in half—width to width.

4. Place the pages of the *All About Me Book* inside the folded construction paper, and staple along the folded edge to make a book.

5. Allow your preschooler to decorate the front cover of his book.

6. When he is finished, open the book and read the pages together pausing on each page to allow him the opportunity to fill in the blanks, draw pictures, or color.

7. When the book is complete, read it as many times as he would like.

LOW PREP *Draw Yourself with Chalk*

Materials:

☐ Chalk

Directions:

1. Ask your preschooler if he would enjoy going outside to draw a chalk person of himself.

2. Invite your preschooler to lie on the sidewalk or in the driveway.

3. Trace an outline around your child.

4. Help him out of the outline, and ask him to color in his chalk person to look like himself with a face, clothes, shoes, etc.

LOW PREP *Measure Body Parts*

Materials:

- ☐ Measure Body Parts Activity Page (Appendix B)
- ☐ Pencil
- ☐ Tape Measure, Unifix Cubes, Crayons, Toys Cars, etc.

Directions:

You may use a tape measure or a different tool to measure body parts. (We enjoyed using Unifix Cubes because you can easily add to and take away from the measurement.) I suggest using the same tool to measure each body part so that you can compare the different lengths.

1. Ask your preschooler to hold up his hand. Place your hand against his hand and explain that your body parts are different sizes. Ask him if he would like to measure the size of his body parts.

2. Show your preschooler the *Measure Body Parts Chart* activity page.

3. Ask him to pick which body part he would like to measure first.

4. Use the measuring tool of choice to determine the length of the body part.

5. Ask your child to write the measurement in the chart. You can write dotted numbers for him to trace, if needed.

6. You can also measure the same body part on your body so that your preschooler can understand that everyone has different size bodies.

7. Continue to measure each body part and write the measurements in the corresponding box on the chart.

Name Collage

Materials:

- ☐ Construction Paper
- ☐ Marker
- ☐ Glue
- ☐ Tissue Paper

Directions:

1. You will need to prepare the activity by drawing your child's name in block letters or bubble letters on construction paper. I recommend using all uppercase letters if your preschooler is at the beginning stages of recognizing letters.

2. Ask your preschooler if he would like to make a collage of his name. Explain to him that a collage is a collection of different colors or materials glued onto a piece of paper.

3. Show him his name. Point to each letter of his name, say the name of the letter, and ask your preschooler to repeat it. After you say the last letter of his name, run your finger across the bottom of his name and say his name out loud.

4. Instruct your preschooler to tear or cut pieces of tissue paper.

5. He will then rub glue onto the letters of his name and place the tissue paper on top of the glue. He can continue this process until his name collage is complete.

6. Find a spot to hang his masterpiece.

`LOW PREP` *Playdough Feelings Faces*

Materials:

- ☐ Playdough Faces Mat Activity Page (Appendix C)
- ☐ Playdough
- ☐ Crayons
- ☐ Sheet Protector

Directions:

1. Explain to your preschooler that everyone makes faces to show how they are feeling. Ask your preschooler if he can demonstrate a happy, sad, mad, silly, scared, or surprised face.

2. Ask him if he would like to create feeling faces using playdough.

3. Give your preschooler the *Playdough Faces Mat* activity page.
   You may choose to give him a girl or a boy face.

4. He can color the face and hair first.

5. Place the activity page inside a sheet protector.

6. Show your preschooler how to create eyes, a nose, and a mouth for the face. For example, you can roll up two balls of playdough and place them in the position of the eyes; create an oval shape for the nose; and roll out a long snake shape and place it in a U-formation to show a happy face.

Apples

ABC Apple Matching

Materials:

- ☐ ABC Apple Activity Page (Appendix D)
- ☐ Circle Label Stickers
- ☐ Marker

Directions:

1. Write the alphabet on the circle label stickers. You can choose whether to write upper or lowercase letters.

   **Suggestion: If your preschooler is new to letter recognition, write all letters in uppercase on the circle label stickers.

2. Show the *ABC Apple Matching* activity page to your preschooler.

3. Explain to him that he will pick a sticker, identify the letter on the sticker, and then place it on the corresponding letter on the apple.

Apple Names

Materials:

- ☐ Apple Name Activity Page (Appendix E)
- ☐ Scissors
- ☐ Marker

Directions:

1. Cut out the basket and number of apples in your child's name from the *Apple Name* activity page.

2. Write your child's name inside the box on the basket. (Write your child's name in all uppercase letters if he is just beginning letter recognition.)

3. Write a single letter from your child's name on each apple you cut out.

4. Explain to your preschooler that he will need to stack the apples in the basket to spell his name. He can use the name on the basket as a guide. (The last letter in your preschooler's name will end at the basket.)

Apple Picking

Materials:

☐ Apples
☐ Painter's Tape
☐ Basket

Directions:

1. Use the painter's tape to tape the design of a big tree onto the floor. You will need to have a tree trunk and branches in various directions.

2. Place an apple on each end of a branch.

3. Explain to your preschooler that he will use the basket to pick apples from a pretend tree today.

4. Ask your preschooler to walk along the taped lines to pick the apples. This will help him develop his gross motor skills.

5. After all of the apples are in the basket you can count them together.

6. Lay the apples back on the tree branches and your child can gather the apples by hopping on one foot, walking backwards on the branches, side stepping, or skipping. All of these are fun, but also help develop the big muscles in his little body.

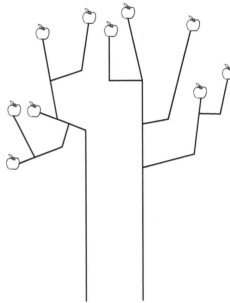

LOW PREP *Apple Printing*

Materials:

☐ Apples
☐ Paper Plate
☐ Construction Paper
☐ Paint
☐ Knife

Directions:

1. Use a knife to cut two apples in half. Cut one apple from the stem down. Cut the other apple across the width of the apple.

2. Ask your child if he would like to investigate the inside of the apple. Let him observe how the inside looks different between the cut apples.

3. Place washable paint on a paper plate.

4. Allow your preschooler to pick a piece of construction paper.

5. Explain that he will use the apples to create a picture. He can place the white part of the apples in the paint and then stamp the apples onto the construction paper.

6. Allow the paint to dry.

LOW PREP *Apple Seed Counting*

Materials:

☐ Apple Seed Counting Activity Page (Appendix F)
☐ Pencil

Directions:

1. Show the *Apple Seed Counting* activity page to your preschooler.

2. Explain to him that he will draw a line from the apple with the number to the apple with the correct number of seeds.

3. Let him try it on his own, but you can help when needed.

LOW PREP *Apple Taste Test*

Materials:

☐ Variety of Apples   ☐ Knife   ☐ Plates

Directions:

1. Purchase four or five different types of apples. Examples include: Gala, Fuji, Golden Delicious, Granny Smith, Honeycrisp, McIntosh, Pink Lady, Kanzi and so many more.

2. Slice the apples.

3. Place a couple of slices of each apple on a plate.
    Each type of apple should have its own plate.

4. Ask your preschooler if he can help you decide which apple tastes the best.

5. Before tasting, ask him to predict which one he thinks will taste the best.

6. Make observations about how each apple is different—look at the color of the apple, smell the apple, touch it, etc.

7. Now let your child taste one apple at a time. Ask him to describe how it tastes (sweet, sour, crunchy, squishy, etc.). Do this for each apple tasted.

8. Let him pick a winner. There is no right or wrong answer!

LOW PREP *Parts of an Apple*

Materials:

☐ Parts of an Apple Activity Page   ☐ Crayons
  (Appendix G)

Directions:

1. Show your preschooler the *Parts of an Apple* activity page.

2. Explain to him that he will color the different parts of the apple.

3. Read the directions to him one at a time, and allow him to color the corresponding part. He can also practice tracing the letters of the word.

4. After he completes all of his coloring, you can cut a real apple in half to allow him to explore the parts he colored on his activity page.

Around the World

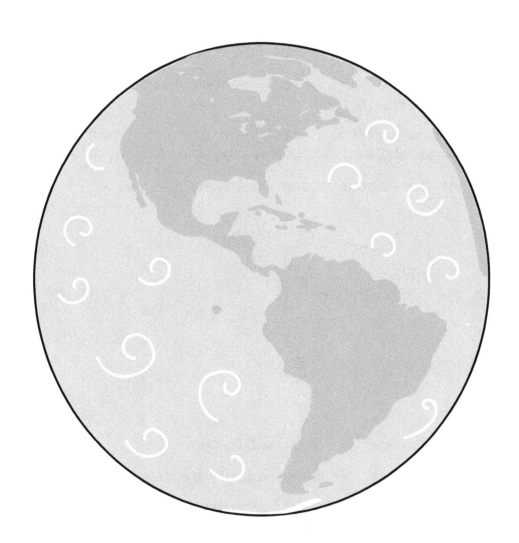

Africa

LOW PREP *Passport*

Materials:

☐ Passport (Appendix H)
☐ Crayons or Markers
☐ Pencil

Directions:

1. Explain to your preschooler that he will be learning about different parts of the world and the people who live there. This week he will learn about Africa.

2. Gather each page of the *Passport* from the Appendix. Cut them in half and staple them together to form a booklet.

3. Assist your child in filling out the personal information. He can either glue a photo of himself or draw a portrait of himself on the page.

4. Show him the continent of Africa on the world map. Ask him to color the image of Africa on the world map in the passport.

5. Turn to the Africa page in the passport. Ask your child to color the continent of Africa.

6. As your child learns about Africa throughout the week, he can fill in his favorite thing he learned about Africa in the box provided.

It is also fun to check out books at the library to learn about special African holidays, animals, the weather, and landforms.

LOW PREP *African Collar Necklace*

Materials:

☐ Paper Plate
☐ Scissors
☐ Paint, Crayons, Markers

Directions:

Women in central African nations have worn beautiful collar necklaces made of metal for hundreds of years. Cloth versions are still worn today.

1. Ask your preschooler if he would like to make a collar necklace.

2. Use scissors to cut a strip to the center of the paper plate.

3. Cut out the inner circle of a paper plate so the outside ribbed edge remains.

4. Ask your preschooler to use crayons, markers, or paint to design his necklace.

5. Your child can proudly wear his new necklace.

Animal Puzzles

Materials:

☐ African Animal Puzzle (Appendix I)
☐ Scissors

Directions:

1. Ask your preschooler if he would enjoy completing a puzzle, that will help him learn what animals live in Africa.

2. Cut out the color pieces of the *African Animal Puzzle*.

3. Place the mixed up pieces in front of your preschooler, as well as the black and white African Animal image.

4. Your preschooler can use the black and white image as a guide to piece the puzzle together by placing the colored puzzle pieces on top of the matching black and white image.

LOW PREP *Build the Nile River*

Materials:

- ☐ 9x13 Aluminum Pan
- ☐ Aluminum Foil
- ☐ Dirt
- ☐ Cup
- ☐ Water
- ☐ African Animals (Optional)
- ☐ Blue Food Coloring (Optional)
- ☐ Grass Seeds (Optional)

Directions:

The Nile River is the longest river in the world.
It is located in Egypt, which is in northeast Africa.

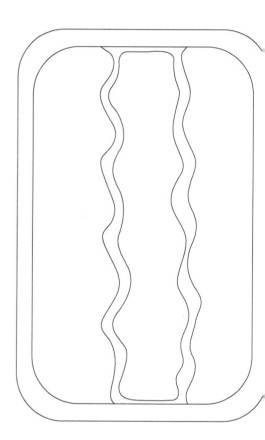

1. Ask your preschooler if he would like to make a small model of the Nile River.

2. Place a 17-inch piece of aluminum foil in the aluminum pan.

3. Ask your preschooler to fold the aluminum foil edges to form a canal in the center of the aluminum pan.

4. Fold the end pieces of the aluminum foil over the lip of the aluminum pan to help the river stay in place.

5. Ask your preschooler to spread dirt on both sides of the aluminum foil river.

6. He can add grass seeds, crocodiles, pyramids, or other African toys to the dirt.

7. Fill a cup with water. Add blue food coloring if desired.

8. Ask your preschooler to pour the water down the Nile River slowly.

9. If he chooses to flood the Nile River, he will be able to learn how the Nile River floods to help the plants along the riverbank grow and flourish.

LOW PREP *Shisima*

Materials:

☐ Shisima Game Board Activity Page (Appendix J)
☐ Piece of Cardboard
☐ Crayons
☐ Scissors
☐ Glue
☐ 3 Game Pieces in One color
☐ 3 Game Pieces in a Different Color

Directions:

This game comes from Kenya in East Africa. Shisima means "body of water" because the center of the game is "water." The game pieces are called impalavali which means "water bugs." Water bugs move very quickly just like Shisima players do during the game.

1. Ask your preschooler if he would like to play a game that many children play in Kenya.

2. Cut out the *Shisima Game Board* activity page.

3. Glue the game board onto a piece of cardboard to make it sturdier.

4. Gather the game pieces for each player.

5. Place the three game pieces on three consecutive points of the octagon across from the other three game pieces.

6. Players take turns moving their game pieces one space. A move must be to an adjacent corner or to the center (shisima). Jumping pieces is not allowed, and there cannot be two pieces on the same space.

7. To win the game, a player must position three of their pieces in a row—including one piece on the shisima.

Antarctica

LOW PREP *Passport*

Materials:

- ☐ Passport (Appendix H)
- ☐ Crayons or Markers
- ☐ Pencil

Directions:

1. Explain to your preschooler that he will continue learning about different parts of the world and the people who live there. This week he will learn about Antarctica.

2. You will continue to use the same passport you created in the Africa activities.

3. Show your preschooler the continent of Antarctica on the world map. Ask him to color the image of Antarctica on the world map in the passport.

4. Turn to the Antarctica page in the passport. Ask your child to color the continent of Antarctica.

5. As your child learns about Antarctica throughout the week, he can fill in his favorite thing he learned about Antarctica in the box provided.

It is also fun to check out books at the library to learn about animals in Antarctica, the weather, and landforms.

LOW PREP *Blubber Experiment*

Materials:

- ☐ Large Bowl
- ☐ Ice Cubes
- ☐ Shortening
- ☐ 2 Plastic Sandwich Bags
- ☐ Duct Tape
- ☐ Food Coloring (Optional)

Directions:

1. Explain to your preschooler that Antarctica is made of snow and ice and water. The water around Antarctica is extremely cold because it has ice floating in it. Ask him how he thinks the penguins, seals or whales that live in Antarctica, are able to stay warm if they don't wear coats.

2. Begin by filling the large bowl half full with water. Your preschooler can add food coloring, if desired.

3. Next, add a layer of ice cubes to the bowl.

4. Let the bowl sit for five minutes, allowing the ice to lower the temperature of the water.

5. Ask your preschooler to briefly place his hand in the water (To prevent discomfort, your child should remove his hand immediately after placing it in water.) Ask him how it feels.

6. Ask your preschooler to help you fill one plastic bag with shortening.

7. Now ask your preschooler to place one hand inside the shortening or blubber bag. Tape the top of the bag so the blubber does not spill out. Squish the blubber around your child's hand.

8. Ask your preschooler to place his other hand inside the empty plastic bag. Seal it with tape.

9. Now place both hands in the icy water.

10. Ask him questions, such as: does one hand feel colder than the other? Why do you think they feel differently?

11. Tell your child that the squishy stuff in the bag represents something called blubber. Blubber is fat that is under an animal's skin or fur. Tell your child it is this blubber that helps keep animals that live in cold places warm. Blubber protects animals from the cold like coats we wear protect us when the temperature outside is cold.

LOW PREP *Snowball Counting*

Materials:

- ☐ Cotton Balls, White Pom Poms, or Mini Marshmallows
- ☐ 2 Bowls
- ☐ Tweezers or Tongs
- ☐ Dice

Directions:

1. Ask your preschooler if he would like to count snowballs.

2. Place a bowl with half a cup of mini marshmallows (pom poms or cotton balls) in front of your preschooler.

3. Ask him to roll a die.

4. He will then count the dots on the die.

5. Instruct him to use his tweezers or tongs to transfer the snowballs from the full bowl to the empty bowl.

   **If your child is younger or new to fine motor skills, it might be easier if he uses just his index finger and thumb to pinch the snowballs. Tongs are for children that struggle to squeeze the small tweezers together. Please use whatever technique (or instrument) that is most appropriate for your child.

6. Your child will continue this process until all snowballs are transferred.

The Ultimate Preschool Activity Guide | Autumn McKay

LOW PREP *Snowflake Building*

Material:

☐ 20 Plastic Straws
☐ Scissors

Directions:

1. Cut the straws at varying lengths. Some of them can be the same lengths.

2. Invite your preschooler to build a snowflake (or a couple of snowflakes).

3. Using the straws he can create a six-sided snowflake, a symmetrical snowflake, or allow him to make his own creation.

LOW PREP *Why Do Ice Cubes Melt?*

Materials:

☐ 5 Ice Cubes   ☐ 5 Small Bowls

Directions:

1. Ask your preschooler to place one ice cube in each of the small bowls.

2. Ask him to place each bowl in a different spot inside or outside the house.

3. Instruct him to continually check each bowl to determine which ice cube melts first.

4. After discovering which ice cube melted first; ask him why he thinks that particular ice cube melted before the other four ice cubes. Explain that many things can make ice melt, and one of those things is heat. Ask your child if he thinks the ice cube that melted the fastest was in a hotter spot?

Asia

LOW PREP *Passport*

Materials:

- ☐ Passport (Appendix H)
- ☐ Crayons or Markers
- ☐ Pencil

Directions:

1. Explain to your preschooler that he will continue learning about different parts of the world and the people who live there. This week he will learn about Asia.

2. You will continue to use the same passport you created in the Africa activities.

3. Show your preschooler the continent of Asia on the world map. Ask him to color the image of Asia on the world map in the passport.

4. Turn to the Asia page in the passport. Ask your child to color the continent of Asia.

5. As your child learns about Asia throughout the week, he can fill in his favorite thing he learned about Asia in the box provided.

You are also encouraged to check out books at the library to learn about the people, animals, the weather, and landforms of Asia.

LOW PREP *Chinese Writing Tray*

Materials:

☐ Chinese Symbols Activity Page (Appendix K)
☐ Tray with Sides
☐ Salt

Directions:

1. Explain to your preschooler that some people speak a different language. China is a country in the continent of Asia. In China, people speak Chinese. Invite him to learn to write Chinese symbols and pronounce a few Chinese words.

2. Pour salt (sand or baking soda) onto a tray with sides.
   You do not need a thick layer of salt.

3. Show your child the *Chinese Symbols* activity page. Point to the first symbol; say the Chinese pronunciation of the symbol and ask your child to repeat it back to you. Now say the word in your native language.

4. Ask your child to attempt to draw the symbol in the salt tray.

5. Do Steps 3 and 4 for all of the Chinese symbols.

LOW PREP *Chopstick Transfer*

Materials:

- ☐ How to Hold Chopsticks Activity Page (Appendix L)
- ☐ Chopsticks
- ☐ Cotton Balls
- ☐ 2 Small Bowls

Directions:

1. Tell your child that the citizens of some countries in Asia use chopsticks to pick up food to eat. Today he will get to attempt to use chopsticks.

2. Show your preschooler how to hold chopsticks. Instructions are located on the *How to Hold Chopsticks* activity page.

3. Place cotton balls in one of the small bowls. Place the empty bowl beside it.

4. Ask your preschooler to transfer the cotton balls from the full bowl to the empty bowl using the chopsticks. This activity might become frustrating if it's difficult for him to hold the chopsticks, but just continue to be an encourager.

LOW PREP   *Japanese Carp Kites*

Materials:

- ☐ Carp Kite Activity Page (Appendix M)
- ☐ Scissors
- ☐ Crayons or Markers
- ☐ Glue
- ☐ Streamers
- ☐ Yarn
- ☐ Hole Puncher

Directions:

1. Tell your preschooler that in Japan, families celebrate a holiday called Children's Day on May 5th each year. During this holiday, families hang a carp kite, called a koinobori, outside their home for each child in the family. Today he will make his own kite.

2. First, ask him to decorate the kite however he pleases.

3. Now, cut out the kite. He can try cutting the image out himself.

4. Next, flip the kite over so that the decorated side is facing down.

5. Glue streamers to the bottom of the fish tail.

6. Flip the fish kite back over, and fold it in half so the decorated kite is showing on both sides.

7. Glue or staple the edges together.

8. Use the hole puncher to place a single hole in the head of the fish.

9. String a piece of yarn through the hole and tie it to form a loop.

10. Allow your preschooler to hang the koinobori kite.

LOW PREP *Make a Chinese Lantern*

Materials:

- ☐ Red Construction Paper
- ☐ Yellow Construction Paper
- ☐ Glue
- ☐ Stapler
- ☐ Scissors

Directions:

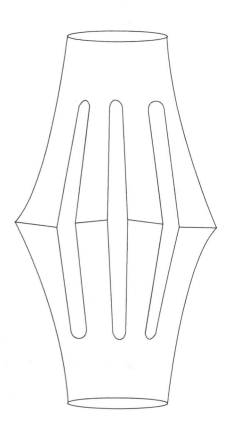

1. Tell your preschooler that people in China hang lanterns during a holiday called Chinese New Year to bring good luck. Today he will have the opportunity to make a lantern.

2. Let your preschooler fold the red construction paper in half, along the length of the paper.

3. He will then use his scissors to cut strips along the crease of the folded, red construction paper. His final cut will need to be at least 2 inches from the edge of the paper.

4. Now your preschooler can cut two 1-inch strips from the yellow construction paper. Cut them along the length of the yellow construction paper.

5. Unfold the red construction paper. Place the paper so that the uncut portions are running along the top and bottom of the page.

6. Glue one yellow strip to the bottom of the uncut red paper.

7. Glue the other yellow strip to the top of the uncut red paper.

8. Wrap your paper in a circle. The crease in the red construction paper should be on the outside of the circle.

9. Staple the edges of the red construction paper together.

10. Cut out a strip from the red construction paper.

11. Staple the red strip across the top opening of the lantern to be a handle.

Australia

LOW PREP *Passport*

Materials:

- ☐ Passport (Appendix H)
- ☐ Crayons or Markers
- ☐ Pencil

Directions:

1. Explain to your preschooler that he will continue learning about different parts of the world and the people who live there. This week he will learn about Australia.

2. You will continue to use the same passport you created in the Africa activities.

3. Show your preschooler the continent of Australia on the world map. Ask him to color the image of Australia on the world map in the passport.

4. Turn to the Australia page in the passport. Ask your child to color the continent of Australia.

5. As your child learns about Australia throughout the week, he can fill in his favorite thing he learned about Australia in the box provided.

You are also encouraged to check out books at the library to learn about the people, animals, the weather, and landforms of this country.

LOW PREP *Aboriginal Boomerang*

Materials:

- ☐ Aboriginal Boomerang Activity Page (Appendix N)
- ☐ Cereal Box or Cardboard
- ☐ Scissors
- ☐ Pencil
- ☐ Paintbrushes
- ☐ Paint

Directions:

1. Explain to your preschooler that Aborigines, which are people that lived in Australia, used boomerangs as hunting weapons. The shape of the boomerang causes the weapon to not be seen when thrown.

2. Cut the boomerang template out from the *Aboriginal Boomerang* activity page.

3. Ask your preschooler to trace the template onto an empty cereal box (or cardboard).

4. Next, cut it out.

5. Now your child can use paint to decorate the boomerang. Allow the boomerang to dry.

LOW PREP *Build a Koala*

Materials:

- ☐ Koala Activity Page (Appendix O)
- ☐ Crayons
- ☐ Glue
- ☐ Scissors
- ☐ Construction Paper

Directions:

1. Tell your preschooler that koalas live in Australia. Koalas are active at night. Koalas have very sharp claws to climb eucalyptus trees and eat their leaves.

2. Show your preschooler the *Koala* activity page. Ask him to color the koala parts.

3. When he is finished coloring, assist him in cutting out the images.

4. Let your child glue the koala together onto a piece of construction paper.

Damper Bread

Materials:

- ☐ 3 Cups of Flour
- ☐ 1 Tablespoon Baking Powder
- ☐ Pinch of Salt
- ☐ ½ to ¾ Cup of Water
- ☐ ¼ Cup of Butter (Cut into Cubes)
- ☐ Baking Sheet
- ☐ Baking Paper
- ☐ Food Processor (Optional)

Directions:

1. Tell your preschooler that together, you and he will make a traditional food that Australians like to eat called damper bread. It's a bread with a crusty exterior and doughy interior.

2. Preheat your oven to 390°F.

3. Line a baking sheet with baking paper and set the baking sheet aside.

4. In your food processor pulse the flour, baking powder, salt, and butter until the mixture resembles fine breadcrumbs. All of the cubes of butter should be mixed through well.

5. Add in ½ cup of water. Pulse the mixture until it comes together. If the mixture is too dry, slowly add the remaining ¼ cup of water using just what is needed to form a dough.

6. Take the mixture out of the food processor and knead until combined, and then shape into mini rolls.

7. Score the top of the dampers with a knife by cutting an "X" into the dough.

8. Bake for 8-10 minutes or until golden and the damper sounds hollow when tapped on the bottom.

9. Serve warm on its own or with butter, maple syrup, honey, or jam.

Kangaroo Name

Materials:

- ☐ Kangaroo Activity Pages (Appendix P)
- ☐ Scissors
- ☐ Marker

Directions:

1. Prepare the activity by writing the letters of your child's name inside the boxes located on the *Kangaroo* activity pages. There should be one letter per box.

2. Cut out the kangaroos on which you have written a letter.

3. Explain to your preschooler that kangaroos live in Australia. They have short front legs, but powerful back legs and a tail to use for jumping. Mother kangaroos have a special pouch on the front of their body to carry their baby, called a joey. Today your child will pretend to be a kangaroo and jump to the letters in his name.

4. Place the kangaroo letters around the floor.

5. Explain that you will ask him to jump to each letter in his name. Ask him what the first letter of his name is, and then jump to it. (You can write your child's name on a piece of paper for him to reference as a guide if needed.)

6. He will continue to call out each letter of his name and jump to it.

7. When he jumps to the last letter, spell his name out loud together with him.

Europe

LOW PREP *Passport*

Materials:

- ☐ Passport (Appendix H)
- ☐ Crayons or Markers
- ☐ Pencil

Directions:

1. Explain to your preschooler that he will continue learning about different parts of the world and the people who live there. This week he will learn about Europe.

2. You will continue to use the same passport you created in the Africa activities.

3. Show your preschooler the continent of Europe on the world map. Ask him to color the image of Europe on the world map in the passport.

4. Turn to the Europe page in the passport. Ask your child to color the continent of Europe.

5. As your child learns about Europe throughout the week, he can fill in his favorite thing he learned about Europe in the box provided.

You are also encouraged to check out books at the library to learn about the people, animals, the weather, and landforms of Europe.

LOW PREP *German Transportation*

Materials:

- ☐ German Transportation Activity Page (Appendix Q)
- ☐ Scissors
- ☐ Brass Fastener

Directions:

1. Invite your preschooler to learn the German translation for different types of transportation.

2. Ask him to cut out the images from the *German Transportation* activity page.

3. Place the smaller circle on top of the larger circle.

4. Help your preschooler place a brass fastener through the center of both circles.

5. He can now spin the small circle to reveal a form of transportation and the German translation of the transportation.

6. Try pronouncing the words together with your child. Have your preschooler repeat it.

LOW PREP *Pouring Tea*

Materials:

- ☐ Tea Pot
- ☐ Tea Cups
- ☐ Water

Directions:

1. Tell your preschooler that in England, a country in Europe, there is a tea time during the afternoon with small sandwiches and snacks. Today he will enjoy his own tea time.

2. Gather a tea pot and tea cups. (I recommend placing a towel underneath the tea set.)

3. Fill the tea pot with water and let your child pour the "tea" into a tea cup. Let him continue as long as he wants to play. This activity helps build coordination.

LOW PREP *Reloj*

Materials:

☐ Deck of Cards

Directions:

1. Tell your preschooler that in Spain, the people in the country play a card game called Reloj (translation: clock), and today you both will get to play. You can play as parent and child or as a family.

2. Remove the joker and queen cards from the card deck, shuffle the cards, and then deal all of the cards face down. (You can start by dealing only 10 cards until your child becomes comfortable with the game.)

3. The first player will flip over his top card from his pile; place it in the middle (discard pile) and say, "Reloj."

4. Going clockwise from the first player, the next player flips over a card and says, "Uno." The game continues moving to the next player who will say, "Dos." As the play moves from player to player, count in this order: Tres (3), Cuatro (4), Cinco (5), Seis (6), Siete (7), Ocho (8), Nueve (9), Diez (10), Sota (Jack), Rey (King).

5. When play of the game progresses to the player who calls out, "rey," the next player will start over with "reloj."

6. If a player flips over a card and says the same number as on the card he flips, he must take the entire discard pile. The game continues by saying the next number in the order.

7. In order to win, you must get rid of all of your cards.

Spaghetti Painting

Materials:

- ☐ 2 Boxes of Spaghetti
- ☐ 6 Rubber Bands
- ☐ Paint
- ☐ Paper

Directions:

1. Explain to your preschooler that people in Italy enjoy making pasta, like spaghetti, and today he will use spaghetti to paint a picture.

2. From each box of spaghetti, bunch 1/3 of the spaghetti together. Tie a rubber band ¼ of the way from the top of each bunch. You should have six total bunches between the two boxes of spaghetti.

3. Boil a pot of water and add a dash of oil.

4. Set the spaghetti bundles in the boiling water with the rubber band away from the water. Let boil for 5-7 minutes.

5. Once done, set the spaghetti bundles out to cool.

6. Allow your preschooler to choose a piece of paper and paint colors to create a painting.

7. Show him how to use the spaghetti paintbrushes to dip in the paint and paint a picture.

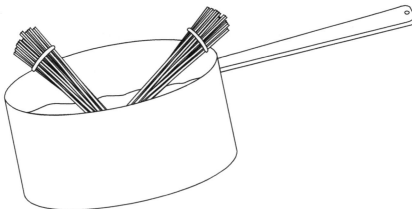

North America

LOW PREP *Passport*

Materials:

- ☐ Passport (Appendix H)
- ☐ Crayons or Markers
- ☐ Pencil

Directions:

1. Explain to your preschooler that he will continue learning about different parts of the world and the people who live there. This week he will learn about North America.

2. You will continue to use the same passport you created in the Africa activities.

3. Show your preschooler the continent of North America on the world map. Ask him to color the image of North America on the world map in the passport.

4. Turn to the North America page in the passport. Ask your child to color the continent of North America.

5. As your child learns about North America throughout the week, he can fill in his favorite thing he learned about North America in the box provided.

You are also encouraged to check out books at the library to learn about the people, animals, the weather, and landforms of this country.

Maple Syrup Playdough

Materials:

- ☐ 2 Cups of All-Purpose Flour
- ☐ 2 Tablespoons Vegetable Oil
- ☐ ½ Cup of Salt
- ☐ 2 Tablespoons of Cream of Tartar
- ☐ 1-1 ½ Cups of Boiling Water
- ☐ 2 Tablespoons of Maple Syrup
- ☐ Mixing Bowl
- ☐ Red Food Coloring (Optional)
- ☐ Red Glitter (Optional)

Directions:

1. Ask your preschooler if he would like to help you make playdough today. Since he is learning about North America this week, he will make maple syrup playdough because Canada makes most of the world's maple syrup.

2. Mix together the flour, salt, cream of tartar, oil, and red glitter in a large mixing bowl.

3. Boil the water. Add the food coloring and maple syrup to the boiling water.

4. Add the boiling water to the dry ingredients. (An adult should complete this step for safety concerns.) Start by adding a cup and add more as needed for playdough consistency.

5. Stir continuously until the mixture becomes a sticky, combined dough.

6. Allow it to cool down. Next, take it out of the bowl and knead the dough vigorously until all of the stickiness has gone.

   **If it remains sticky, add a pinch of flour.

7. Allow your preschooler to smell the playdough and play with it.

LOW PREP *North America Maze*

Materials:

- ☐ North America Maze Activity Page (Appendix R)
- ☐ Pencil

Directions:

1. Show your preschooler the *North America Maze* activity page.

2. Ask your child if he can use his finger to move from the top of North America to the bottom without crossing any lines.

3. Now he can use his pencil to successfully get through the maze.

Pull Open Pinata

Materials:

- ☐ Toilet Paper Tube
- ☐ Ribbon
- ☐ Scissors
- ☐ Tape
- ☐ Tissue Paper
- ☐ Glue
- ☐ Treats

Directions:

1. Tell your preschooler that in Mexico people celebrate a holiday called Cinco de Mayo. This holiday is celebrated because it's the day Mexico won a battle against France in the battle of Puebla in 1862. This holiday has become popular in the United States too. People who celebrate the holiday might have piñatas. A piñata is a decorated shape that contains treats inside. People often use sticks to hit them open.

2. Today your preschooler will get to make a piñata that he can pull open. Allow your preschooler to decorate the toilet paper tube with tissue paper, crayons, markers, paint, etc.

3. When he has finished decorating, cut a piece of ribbon 6 inches long.

4. Tape both ends of the ribbon to the inside of the top of toilet paper tube to form a handle.

5. Cut a 3-inch square piece of tissue paper. Cut a small ¾ inch wide "X" in the center of the square tissue paper.

6. Glue the square to the bottom of the toilet paper tube.

7. Place lightweight treats (balloons, plastic animals, a candy, etc.) inside the top of the piñata.

8. Cut a piece a ribbon 10 inches long. Tape it to the "X" on the bottom of the piñata.

9. Hang the piñata. Allow your preschooler to pull the ribbon to release the treats of his piñata

LOW PREP *Scrap Paper Sombreros*

Materials:

- ☐ Sombrero Activity Page (Appendix S)
- ☐ Glue
- ☐ Scrap Paper

Directions:

1. Explain to your preschooler that when visiting Mexico he might see people wearing sombreros. Sombreros are really big hats that help protect a person's face and skin from the sun.

2. Show your preschooler the *Sombrero* activity page. Explain that he will tear up pieces of paper and glue them to the sombrero to create a design.

3. Allow your preschooler to tear up pieces of paper—any colors he chooses.

   **Tearing paper allows your preschooler to build the small muscles in his fingers that are needed to help grip a pencil properly.

4. After he tears the paper he needs, he will need to spread glue on the *Sombrero* activity page. Now place the scraps of paper as desired.

South America

LOW PREP *Passport*

Materials:

- ☐ Passport (Appendix H)
- ☐ Crayons or Markers
- ☐ Pencil

Directions:

1. Explain to your preschooler that he will continue learning about different parts of the world and the people who live there. This week he will learn about South America.

2. You will continue to use the same passport you created in the Africa activities.

3. Show your preschooler the continent of South America on the world map. Ask him to color the image of South America on the world map in the passport.

4. Turn to the South America page in the passport. Ask your child to color the continent of South America.

5. As your child learns about South America throughout the week, he can fill in his favorite thing he learned about South America in the box provided.

You are encouraged to check out books at the library to learn about the people, animals, the weather, and landforms of South America.

LOW PREP **Country Syllable Count**

Materials:
☐ Country Syllable Count Activity Page (Appendix T)
☐ Pom Poms

Directions:

1. Explain to your preschooler that South America is called a continent. The continent of South America is divided into countries. Each country inside South America has its own name, and today he will learn the names of each country and count the syllables in the name.

   **An excellent technique to use in counting syllables in a word is to have your child place his hand under his chin. Have your child say a word slowly. Each time his chin drops down, that is a syllable. For example, the word "Brazil" has two syllables "Bra-zil."

2. Show your preschooler the *Country Syllable Count* activity page.

3. Point to the first country. Say the name of the country to your child. Show him the flag.

4. Now ask him to place his hand under his chin and say the country's name slowly to count the syllables.

5. Ask your child how many syllables he counted. Complete Step 4 together if his answer is incorrect.

6. Ask him to place a pom pom on the correct number of syllables he counted in the country's name.

7. Do this for each country in South America.

LOW PREP *Living vs. Nonliving in South America*

Materials:

- ☐ Living vs. Nonliving Activity Page (Appendix U)
- ☐ Scissors
- ☐ Glue

Directions:

1. Tell your preschooler that there are things that are alive and things that are not alive. Things that are alive or living can grow, make babies, and eat. Together you will look at some pictures of things in South America and decide if they are living or nonliving.

2. Show your preschooler the *Living vs. Nonliving* activity page. Look at each picture at the bottom of the activity page.

3. Ask your preschooler to cut out the pictures.

4. Ask him to pick up a picture, identify what it is, and determine if it is living or nonliving.

5. When he states the answer, ask him why he believes that item to be living or nonliving. This will help him be able to explain his thought process, which is a good skill to have throughout life.

6. Let him glue the picture in the correct column on the chart.

7. Continue Steps 4-6 until complete.

Paper Chain Snake Patterns

Materials:

☐ Construction Paper (3 Colors)
☐ Scissors
☐ Stapler

Directions:

1. Hold your construction paper landscape-oriented. Cut strips from each color of construction paper. (You might need more than one piece of each color depending on how many snakes your preschooler wants to make.)

2. Explain to your preschooler that the Amazon Rainforest is located in South America. Many animals live in the Amazon Rainforest, including all kinds of snakes. Today he will have the opportunity to make snakes. He will construct his snakes by creating a repeating pattern.

3. Using the strips of paper show your preschooler a pattern. Place color A, color B, color A, and color B in front of your child. Explain the pattern, and ask him what color would appear next in the pattern. Do this again with color A, color B, color C, and repeat.

4. Ask your child to select a color to begin the multi colored pattern of his snake. Show him how to wrap the strip into a circle and staple it together.

5. He can draw eyes and a tongue on his snake's head.

6. Ask your preschooler what color comes next in his pattern. Show him how to wrap the strip of paper through the first circle and staple it together so that that the two circles create a chain.

7. Continue the pattern as long as your preschooler would like. He can even create another snake using a different pattern.

Zamponas

Materials:

☐ 8 Plastic Smoothie Straws
☐ Scissors
☐ Tape

Directions:

1. Ask your preschooler if he would like to create an instrument used in South America. It is called a Zampona. It is a panpipe made of hollow reeds of differing lengths.

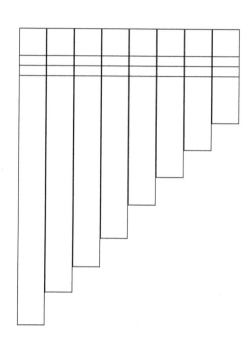

2. Cut the straws in these lengths: 1 ½ inches, 2 ½ inches, 3 ½ inches, 4 ½ inches, 5 ½ inches, 6 ½ inches, 7 ½ inches, and 8 ½ inches.

3. Ask your preschooler to line the straws up from smallest to biggest.

4. Make sure the ends of each straw are even, and then lay a piece of tape across all eight straws.

5. Flip the straws over; lay a piece of tape across the back of all eight straws.

6. Now wrap a piece of tape around all of the straws. It should go over the previous tape.

7. Ask your preschooler to hold the Zampona below his bottom lip and blow across the straws. He can move the Zampona back and forth across his bottom lip to create different sounds.

Bees

Add and Subtract Bees

Materials:

☐ Add and Subtract Bee Activity Page (Appendix V)
☐ Scissors
☐ Laminator (Optional)

Directions:

1. Cut out each yellow hexagon and bumblebee from the *Add and Subtract Bee* activity page. (Optional: Laminate the activity page prior to cutting out the images to increase the durability of the pieces.)

2. Ask your preschooler if he would like to build a beehive.

3. Explain to him that you will call out a number (Step 4). Using that number, he will count out a corresponding number of honeycombs (yellow hexagons) and create a beehive with the honeycombs.

4. Call out a number for him to begin to build his beehive. (Ex. 10 honeycombs)

5. Now, explain to him that some bees in the beehive make the honey while other bees go out to search for pollen. Tell your child you will give him a certain number of bees to place inside his constructed beehive.

6. Ask him to place a certain number of bees inside the beehive. (Ex. 5 bees)

7. To practice addition, ask your preschooler how many more bees need to bring pollen to the beehive to fill the beehive. (Ex. 5 bees)

8. Say the addition sentence out loud to him, "__ bees + __ bees = how many bees?" Allow him to count the total number of bees to answer the question. (Ex. 5 bees + 5 bees = 10 bees)

9. To practice subtraction, ask your preschooler to fly a certain number of bees out of the beehive to look for pollen. (Ex. 2 bees)

10. Say the subtraction sentence out loud to him, "__ bees - __ bees = how many bees?" Allow him to count the total number of bees inside the beehive to answer the question. (Ex. 5 bees – 2 bees = 3 bees)

11. Create new addition and subtraction problems for your child to solve.

The Ultimate Preschool Activity Guide | Autumn McKay

LOW PREP *Bee Life Cycle*

Materials:

- ☐ Bee Life Cycle Activity Page (Appendix W)
- ☐ Scissors
- ☐ Crayons
- ☐ Glue

Directions:

1. Ask your preschooler if he would like to learn how a bumblebee grows up.

2. Show him the *Bee Life Cycle* activity page.

3. Ask him to color the pictures.

4. Tell your child he can cut out the pictures at the bottom of the activity page.

5. Explain to him that a bumblebee starts out inside an egg, just like a bird. Show him the egg picture he needs to cut out.

6. Next, show him the larva picture. Explain that once the egg hatches a worm looking creature called a larva appears. The larva eats royal jelly (a secretion from the honey bee to nourish the larva) for three days and then the larva eats honey and pollen.

7. The larva grows into a pupa. The pupa grows tiny wings, legs, and other bumblebee parts. The pupa will nibble out of the wax cell. Show him the pupa picture he cut out.

8. Now show your child the adult bee picture. Tell him that after the pupa has eaten its way out of the wax cell it grows into a bumblebee that works inside the bee hive or gathers pollen.

9. Point to the box at the top of the Bee Life Cycle activity page and ask your preschooler which picture came first in the bee's life. Ask him to glue the egg picture in the box.

10. Continue this until each picture is glued in place.

LOW PREP *Bee Mask*

Materials:

- ☐ Bee Mask Activity Page (Appendix X)
- ☐ Scissors
- ☐ Crayons
- ☐ Stapler
- ☐ String

Directions:

1. Ask your preschooler if he would like to be a bumblebee.

2. Show your preschooler the *Bee Mask* activity page. Ask him to color the bee mask.

3. When your child has finished coloring the mask, he may cut the mask out. You may need to assist him in cutting out the eyes.

4. Cut a string that will fit around your child's head.

5. Staple one end of the string to the right bee eye. Staple the other end of the string to the left bee eye.

6. Slide the mask onto your preschooler's head and allow him to pretend to be a bee.

LOW PREP *Bee Pollen Counting*

Materials:

- ☐ Empty Egg Carton Bottom
- ☐ Yellow Pom Poms
- ☐ Tweezers or Tongs
- ☐ 2 Dice

Directions:

1. Ask your preschooler if he would like to be a bumblebee that collects pollen.

2. Place the egg carton bottom, yellow pom poms, dice, and tweezers in front of your preschooler.

3. Ask him to roll the dice and count the number on the dice.

4. Instruct him to use the tweezers to pick up the same number of yellow pom poms (pollen) to place inside the beehive. One pollen should be placed inside each egg cup.

5. When he is done, he can dump the pollen out and start again.

LOW PREP *Bumblebee Number Line*

Materials:

☐ Add and Subtract Bee Activity Page (Appendix V)
☐ Dry Erase Marker

Directions:

1. Use the yellow hexagons and a bumblebee from the *Add and Subtract Bees* activity. Gather 10 yellow hexagons. Using the Expo marker, write the numbers one through ten on the hexagons. Line the hexagons up in a number line.

2. Ask your preschooler to come help the bumblebee fly from number to number.

3. Hand your child a bumblebee. Ask him to start on a number. (Ex. 1)

4. Ask him to fly his bumblebee to another number and count how many numbers he flies over to get there. (Ex. Fly to 7. How many numbers does the bumblebee fly over to get from 1 to 7?)

5. Say the addition sentence together with your preschooler. (Ex. 1+6=7)

6. To practice subtraction, the bumblebee will start at higher numbers and fly to lower numbers. Then repeat Step 4.

7. Do this as many times as your child would enjoy.

LOW PREP *Flying Bee Cutting*

Materials:

☐ Flying Bee Cutting Activity Page (Appendix Y)
☐ Scissors

Directions:

1. Show your preschooler the *Flying Bee Cutting* activity page. Explain that the bees need help getting back to their beehive. Ask your preschooler if he can cut along the lines to guide the bee back to the beehive.

2. Show your preschooler how to properly hold scissors—thumb should be on top and the fingers should be on bottom. While holding the scissors correctly, ask him to practice opening and closing the scissors. This takes a lot of concentration and coordination from the fine muscles of him hand, so cheer him on as he does it.

3. Allow your preschooler to cut along each dotted line. The lines increase in difficulty, so if cutting is new to your child you might need to assist him with holding and turning the paper so he can focus on the cutting motion.

LOW PREP *Label Parts of a Bee*

Materials:

- ☐ Label Parts of a Bee Activity Page (Appendix Z)
- ☐ Scissors
- ☐ Glue
- ☐ Crayons

Directions:

1. Show your preschooler the *Label Parts of a Bee* activity page. Ask him if he would like to learn the body parts of a bee.

2. First, ask him to color the picture of the bee.

3. Next, ask your child to cut out the words at the bottom of the activity page.

4. Read the words together. Ask him if he can identify where each body part is located on the bee and place the word in the correct box.

   The thorax is the middle section of the bee, and the abdomen is the big section of the bee with the stinger.

5. After he has placed each label in the correct box, ask your child to glue the labels in place.

Nectar Relay

Materials:

- ☐ Cup
- ☐ Eye Dropper
- ☐ Ice Cube Tray
- ☐ Yellow Food Coloring (Optional)

Directions:

1. Ask your preschooler if he would enjoy pretending to be "a bee" collecting nectar and pollen from flowers.

2. Set up the relay race by filling a cup with water. Squirt two to three drops of yellow food coloring in the water. Place the cup of water on one side of the yard. Place the ice cube tray ten feet away from the cup of water. Hand your preschooler the eye dropper. Ask your preschooler to stand beside the cup of water.

3. Instruct your child to use the eye dropper to soak up the nectar (yellow water) from the cup.

4. Next, he will run to the beehive (ice cube tray) and fill the honeycomb with the nectar.

5. In order to win, he must fill each honeycomb with nectar.

6. This is a fun activity to do with more than one person; so, siblings, parents, or grandparents are welcome to race against the preschooler.

The Ultimate Preschool Activity Guide | Autumn McKay

Paper Bag Bumblebee

Materials:

- ☐ White Paper Lunch Bag
- ☐ Yellow Paint
- ☐ Paintbrush
- ☐ Black Construction Paper
- ☐ 2 White Doilies

- ☐ Black Marker
- ☐ Black Pipe Cleaner
- ☐ Scissors
- ☐ Glue
- ☐ Tape

Directions:

1. Ask your preschooler if he would enjoy making a bumblebee puppet.

2. Ask your preschooler to paint the paper lunch bag yellow. Let it dry completely.

3. While the bag is drying, cut four 1-inch strips from your black construction paper for the bee's stripes.

4. Once the bag is dry, ask your preschooler to glue the stripes onto your paper bag underneath the flap. It should make a pattern of yellow and black.

5. Fold one side of the doilies in approximately an inch to make a straight edge. Flip the bag over and tape the doilies to either side of the paper bag to make the wings.

6. Cut the black pipe cleaner in half. Twirl each pipe cleaner around your finger to curl them. Tape each pipe cleaner to the back of the bee, at the top, to make antennae.

7. Flip the paper bag back over. Ask your preschooler to draw eyes and a mouth on the flap of the puppet.

8. Your preschooler can now fly his bee around.

Stripe Counting

Materials:

- ☐ Stripe Counting Activity Page (Appendix AA)
- ☐ Crayons or Do-A-Dot Markers

Directions:

1. Show your preschooler the *Stripe Counting* activity page.

2. Point to the first bumblebee on the activity page. Ask your preschooler to count the stripes on the bumblebee.

3. Next, ask him to color or place a dot on the number that matches the number of stripes he counted.

4. Do this for each bumblebee on the activity page.

Bears

Bear Hunt Sequence

Materials:

- ☐ *We're Going on a Bear Hunt* by Michael Rosen
- ☐ 6 Pieces of Paper
- ☐ Markers

Directions:

1. Draw each scene from the *We're Going on a Bear Hunt* book onto a piece of paper. (Even if you are not a great artist, you can do it! Your drawings do not have to be detailed scenes—just simple. For instance, the grass field can be just green lines across the piece of paper.)

2. After you have drawn your scenes, invite your preschooler to come read *We're Going on a Bear Hunt* with you.

3. As you read the story, show him the pictures you drew that match the scene in the story.

4. After you have read the story, ask him to go on a bear hunt with you. Explain that your hunt will be just like the bear hunt in the book; so, before he can begin the hunt he will need to place the pictures in the correct order of the hunt.

5. Ask him where the bear hunt first began in the book. You can help provide him with clues if necessary. Ask him to lay the grass field picture on the floor.

6. Continue Step 5 until each scene is laid on the floor.

7. Start at the grass field scene. Recite the lines from the book. Then ask your preschooler to pretend to walk through the grass field to get to the next scene.

8. Continue Step 7 for each scene.

9. When you "arrive at" the bear cave picture and encounter the pretend bear, quickly run back through each picture scene you drew.

The Ultimate Preschool Activity Guide | Autumn McKay

LOW PREP *Bear Patterns*

Materials:

☐ Bear Patterns Activity Page (Appendix AB)
☐ Scissors
☐ Glue

Directions:

1. Show your preschooler the *Bear Patterns* activity page. Explain that some of the bears went looking for berries and became separated from their families. Tell your child that he needs to help the lost bears find their way back to the correct family by completing the pattern.

2. Ask your preschooler to cut out the bears at the bottom of the page.

   I recommend cutting the patterns into strips because this helps your child to be able to focus on one pattern at a time.

3. Pick a pattern. Point to the colored bears on the pattern as you say the pattern out loud to your child. Have him repeat the pattern to you.

4. Ask him which colored bear he thinks comes next in the pattern. Praise him if he gets it right. If he is incorrect, say the pattern again with him and help him with the answer.

5. Ask your preschooler to glue the bear in place.

6. Now, ask him to tell you the next bear in the pattern.

7. Glue this bear in place too.

8. Complete Steps 3-7 for each pattern.

Bear Paw Names

Materials:

- ☐ Bear Paw Activity Page (Appendix AC)
- ☐ Scissors
- ☐ Marker

Directions:

1. Cut out enough bear paws for your child's name from the *Bear Paw* activity page.

2. Write each letter of his name on a separate paw.

   **Start with only uppercase letters if your child is just beginning to learn letters.

3. Lay the bear paws on a flat surface and mix them up.

4. Invite your preschooler to come spell his name.

5. Ask your preschooler to locate the first letter of his name. When he finds it, place it on the left-hand side of the table.

6. Ask him to find the next letter, and then place it beside the previous letter.

7. Continue to find each letter until his name is spelled out.

8. Say each letter as you point to it, and slide your finger underneath the name as you read the name.

9. Ask him to complete Step 8 with you.

Feed the Bear

Materials:

- ☐ Fish Activity Page (Appendix AD)
- ☐ Scissors
- ☐ Brown Paper Lunch Bag
- ☐ Black Marker

Directions:

1. Draw a bear face on the paper lunch bag.

2. Cut out a mouth on the bear face so your preschooler can insert the fish.

3. Cut out enough fish from the *Fish* activity page to spell your child's name.

4. Write each letter of his name on a separate fish.

   **Start with only uppercase letters if your child is just beginning to learn letters.

5. Invite your preschooler to come feed the bear.

6. Lay the fish in front of your child. Ask him to find the first letter of his name. When he does, he can feed the fish to the bear.

7. Continue until each fish is fed to the bear.

Gummy Bear Science

Materials:

- ☐ 2 Gummy Bears
- ☐ 2 Clear Cups
- ☐ Water

Directions:

1. Ask your preschooler if he would like to do an experiment with gummy bears.

2. Place a clear, empty cup in front of your preschooler. Place a clear cup that is half full with water in front of your preschooler.

3. Hand him a gummy bear. Let him use his five senses to investigate the gummy bear.

4. Explain that one gummy bear will be placed in the empty cup for one day while the other gummy bear will be placed in the cup of water for one day.

5. Ask him to guess what he thinks will happen to each gummy bear. Explain that there is not a wrong answer.

6. Allow him to place each gummy bear in its respected cup.

7. Place the cups in a place that will not be disturbed.

8. After 24 hours, come back to the gummy bears. Take them out of the cups.

9. Let your child investigate the differences between the two gummy bears. Ask him questions about his observations and thoughts.

10. Explain to him that the gummy bear in the water cup absorbed the water. The water moved from the cup into the gummy bear which made the bear "grow."

LOW PREP ‹ *Make a Bear Cave*

Materials:

☐ Pillows ☐ Blankets ☐ Couch Cushions

Directions:

1. Explain to your preschooler that bears make their home inside caves. This is where bears like to hibernate or sleep during the winter. Today he will have the opportunity to make a bear cave.

2. Allow your child to use pillows, blankets, couch cushions, etc. to create an awesome bear cave to play inside.

3. Join your preschooler inside the cave. Eat lunch or read books together inside the cave.

LOW PREP ‹ *Teddy Bear More or Less*

Materials:

☐ Teddy Bear More or Less Activity Page (Appendix AE)
☐ Teddy Grahams or Counters
☐ 2 Dice

Directions:

1. Show your preschooler the *Teddy Bear More or Less* activity page.

2. Ask him to roll both dice and count the number on the dice.

3. Using the number obtained from rolling the dice (Step 2), place the same amount of teddy grahams in the first column on the activity page. One teddy graham per box.

4. Ask him to roll the dice again, and count the number on the dice.

5. Using the number obtained from rolling the dice (Step 4), place the same amount of teddy grahams in the second column on the activity page. One teddy graham per box.

6. Ask your child which column has more teddy grahams. State the sentence to him, "X is more than X."

7. Repeat Steps 2-6 as many times as your child would enjoy.

Birds

Bird Sorting

Materials:

- ☐ Bird Sorting Activity Page (Appendix AF)
- ☐ 3 Brown Paper Lunch Bags
- ☐ Scissors

Directions:

1. Create a nest from each paper lunch bag by first cutting the top half of the bag off. Next, roll the edges of the bag down towards the inside of the bag.

2. Cut out each bird from the *Bird Sorting* activity page.

3. Invite your preschooler to join you in sorting the birds.

4. Place the nests and birds in front of your preschooler. Tell him that the first nest belongs to the small birds, the second nest belongs to the medium size birds, and the third nest belongs to the big birds.

5. Ask him to fly each sized bird to its correct sized nest.

LOW PREP # Birdseed Writing

Materials:

- ☐ Birdseed
- ☐ Cookie Tray
- ☐ Flashcards (Optional)

Directions:

1. Pour a thin layer of birdseed onto a cookie tray.

2. Tell your preschooler that birds enjoy eating seeds and nuts like the ones found on the cookie tray. Today he will have the opportunity to write numbers and letters in the birdseed.

3. Place a number or letter flashcard in front of your child and ask him to write it in the birdseed.

4. If you do not have flashcards, simply write a number or letter in the birdseed and ask your child to write the same letter or number. It is always fun to help your child write the letters of his name.

LOW PREP *Feather Cutting*

Materials:

- ☐ Feather Activity Page (Appendix AG)
- ☐ Scissors

Directions:

1. Tell your preschooler that a bird's body is covered with feathers. Today he will get to cut out feathers.

   **To add some fun to this activity, print the Feather activity page out on colored paper.

2. Show him the *Feather* activity page.

3. If your child is comfortable enough with scissors, allow him to cut the feathers out himself. However, if he is still mastering scissor skills, cut the feathers out and allow your child to cut along the edges to make a frayed feather.

LOW PREP *Feather Painting*

Materials:

- ☐ Feathers
- ☐ Paint
- ☐ Paper

Directions:

1. Ask your preschooler if he would enjoy painting a picture. Tell your child that instead of using paintbrushes he will use feathers.

2. Allow your child to pick four colors of paint. Squirt the paint onto a paper plate. Place a feather in each paint color.

3. Allow him to paint a picture onto his paper using the feathers.

4. Let the painting dry before hanging it up.

Paper Plate Bird

Materials:

- ☐ 2 Paper Plates
- ☐ Scissors
- ☐ Yellow Construction Paper
- ☐ Glue
- ☐ Paint
- ☐ Tissue Paper
- ☐ Stapler (Optional)

Directions:

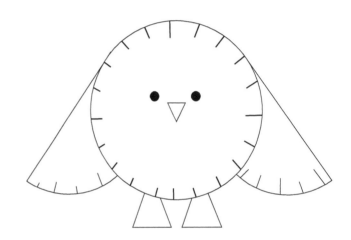

1. Ask your preschooler if he would enjoy making a bird.

2. Cut one paper plate in half.

3. Allow your preschooler to paint the paper plates (the whole plate and the one you cut in half).

4. While he is painting, cut out a medium sized diamond from the yellow construction paper and two medium triangles. This will be the beak and feet for the bird.

5. Fold the diamond in half so that it forms a triangle.

6. When your preschooler is finished painting the plates, he may stick tissue paper squares onto the wet paint if he pleases. The tissue paper represents feathers.

7. After the paint and tissue paper is dry, it is time to assemble the bird. First, place the whole paper plate in front of your child. Place the half circles on either side of the paper plate—straight edge facing away from preschooler.

8. Staple or glue the half circles to the back of the paper plate. These are the wings.

9. Let your preschooler glue or staple the two medium triangles to the bottom, underside of the bird—the whole plate. These are the feet.

10. Allow your preschooler to rub glue on one triangle of the diamond. Place the glued triangle in the center of the plate to be the bird's beak.

11. Let your preschooler draw eyes above the beak to complete the bird.

LOW PREP *Parts of a Bird*

Materials:

- ☐ Parts of a Bird Activity Page (Appendix AH)
- ☐ Crayons
- ☐ Scissors
- ☐ Glue

Directions:

1. Show your child the *Parts of a Bird* activity page.

2. Ask him to cut out the words on the activity page.

3. After he cuts out the words, read one bird part word to your child and ask him where the part is located on the bird.

4. When he places it on the correct part, let him glue it in place.

5. Continue Steps 3 and 4 until all of the bird parts are labeled.

6. Let your preschooler color the bird.

Body Systems

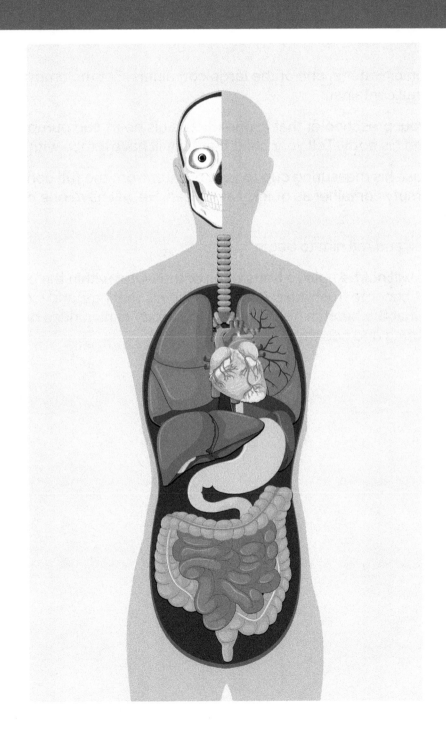

Circulatory

LOW PREP *Beat the Clock*

Materials:

- ☐ 2 Large Containers
- ☐ ¼ Measuring Cup
- ☐ Gallon of Water
- ☐ Timer

Directions:

1. Pour a gallon of water in one of the large containers. Set the empty container beside the full container.

2. Explain to your preschooler that in one minute his heart can pump 1.3 gallons of blood around his body. Tell your child that he will have a race with his heart.

3. Ask him to use his measuring cup to scoop water from the full container and pour it into the empty container as quickly as he can. He will have one minute to fill the container.

4. Set the timer, and tell him to begin.

It is likely that he will not be able to transfer all of the water within the one minute time limit, so he might become frustrated. Acknowledge his feelings, and explain to him how grateful you are that the heart in his body and your body can work so hard every day to keep you both strong and healthy.

Blood Bottle

Materials:

- ☐ Plastic Water Bottle
- ☐ Yellow Food Coloring
- ☐ Red Food Coloring
- ☐ Ziploc Bag
- ☐ Cheerios
- ☐ Mini Marshmallows
- ☐ Purple Pom Poms

Directions:

1. Before the activity, pour one or two handfuls of Cheerios into a Ziploc bag. Add five drops of red food coloring. Seal the bag and shake it up so that the Cheerios turn red.

2. Ask your preschooler if he wants to see what is inside blood.

3. Hand your child a plastic water bottle. Let him fill the bottle halfway up with water.

4. Let him add three drops of yellow food coloring to the water. Explain that this is the plasma. Plasma carries water, salt, and minerals all over the body.

5. Now let your preschooler add the red Cheerios to the plasma. Add a large amount. The Cheerios will turn the plasma (yellow water) red. The Cheerios represent the red blood cells. The red blood cells (Cheerios) carry oxygen from the lungs to the body and carbon dioxide back to the lungs.

6. Let your preschooler add a few mini marshmallows to the bottle. The mini marshmallows represent white blood cells. White blood cells (mini marshmallows) fight germs that invade the body.

7. Let your preschooler add purple pom poms to the bottle. The purple pom poms represent platelets. Platelets (purple pom poms) help the blood clot. Tell your child that when his blood clots, it stops the bleeding that occurs when he "gets a boo boo."

8. Put the top on the water bottle and allow your preschooler to explore the "blood."

LOW PREP *Circulatory Coloring*

Materials:

☐ Circulatory Coloring Activity Page (Appendix AI)
☐ Crayons

Directions:

1. Show your preschooler the *Circulatory Coloring* activity page.

2. Ask your preschooler to draw a face and hair on each figure on the activity page.

3. Explain to your preschooler that there are four chambers of the heart. Two chambers help pump blood with oxygen to all the parts of the body and the other two chambers help bring blood back from the body after it has delivered the blood with oxygen.

4. Point to the body on the left side of the activity page. Tell your preschooler that arteries carry blood with oxygen to the body parts. Ask him to color the arteries on the left body red.

5. Point to the body on the right side of the activity page. Tell your child that veins carry blood back to the heart from the body parts. Ask him to color the veins on the right body blue.

6. Explain to your preschooler that arteries and veins are both inside the same body, but it's easier to see the veins and arteries when they are separated in different pictures.

LOW PREP *Heart Pump*

Materials:

- ☐ Mason Jar
- ☐ Balloon
- ☐ Bendable Straws
- ☐ Scissors
- ☐ Toothpick
- ☐ Water
- ☐ Tape
- ☐ Large Pan
- ☐ Red Food Coloring (Optional)

Directions:

1. Ask your preschooler to help you make a heart.

2. Fill the mason jar half full with water.

3. Ask your preschooler to drop three drops of red food coloring into the water.

4. Cut the neck of the balloon off at the part where it starts to widen into a balloon. Set the neck part aside.

5. Stretch the balloon over the opening of the jar, pulling it down as tightly as you can. The flatter the surface of the balloon, the better.

6. Use the tip of the toothpick to poke two holes in the stretched surface of the balloon. Make the holes one to two inches apart from each other and near opposite edges of the jar.

7. Ask your preschooler to stick the long part of the straw into each hole of the stretched balloon. The straws should fit securely in the holes so no air can get through around the straws.

8. Ask your preschooler to slide the cut end of the balloon neck onto one of the straws and lightly tape it around the straw. This will act as a flap, like the valves in the heart.

9. Set the pump in a large pan to catch the pumped water.

10. Bend the straws downward.

11. Gently press in the center of the stretched balloon and watch the water come up through the straw and squirt out.

12. Allow your preschooler to test out the heart pump. Explain that this pump is like one of the chambers in his heart. The covered straw is like a valve in the heart. It keeps blood that has been pumped into the chamber from going back out to the chamber it came from so that each chamber can work the correct way.

LOW PREP *Measure Heart Beat*

Materials:

☐ Toothpick
☐ Mini Marshmallow

☐ Timer

Directions:

1. Ask your preschooler if he would enjoy seeing his heart beat.

2. Tell him to place his hand over his chest to feel his heart beat. Explain that his heart is in his chest, but there are different areas on his body where he can feel his heart beat or pulse. Show him how to point his index finger and middle finger together and place them on the side of his neck to feel his pulse. Take the same two fingers and try to locate his pulse in his wrist.

3. Ask him to place a toothpick into a mini marshmallow (not all the way through).

4. Now, ask him to place his hand, palm up, onto the table.

5. Using your index finger and middle finger try to locate his pulse in his wrist. It should be in the wrist below the thumb.

6. Place the mini marshmallow on top of the pulse.

7. Allow your preschooler to observe the toothpick as it raises and lowers as his heart beats.

8. Set a timer for one minute. Ask your preschooler to help you count how many times his heart beats (the toothpick raises up) during that one minute.

Digestive

LOW PREP *Digest Food Experiment*

Materials:

- ☐ Quart Size Ziploc Bag
- ☐ Marker
- ☐ 3 Crackers
- ☐ Clear Soda

Directions:

1. Ask your preschooler if he would enjoy seeing how his stomach breaks food apart so he can receive the nutrients to make him strong and healthy.

2. Use the marker to draw the outline of a stomach on the Ziploc bag. The stomach looks like an oval with a tube coming in from the top and a tube going out to the side.

3. Ask your child to pretend that he just ate three crackers. Ask him to place the crackers in the bag. Seal the bag.

4. Explain to your child that first the stomach breaks down food by squeezing and moving the food. Ask your preschooler to use his hands to be the stomach and crush the crackers into small pieces.

5. Tell him that the stomach also uses liquids (stomach acid) to break down food. Open the sealed bag. Ask your preschooler to pour ½ a cup of clear soda into the bag. Seal the bag again.

6. With the stomach acid, the stomach continues to squeeze and move the food around to break the food down into smaller pieces. Ask your preschooler to continue to use his hands to be the stomach muscles that squeeze and move the food.

7. Ask your child to observe what happened to the crackers. Ask him questions about the experiment. Did the food break down more with or without the acid? Why does the body need to break down food?

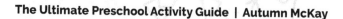

🏷 LOW PREP *Digestive Tract Sequencing*

Materials:

- ☐ Digestive Activity Page (Appendix AJ)
- ☐ Crayons

Directions:

1. Show your preschooler the *Digestive* activity page. Tell him that you will tell him about how he digests food and he will color each step the correct color.

2. Ask him to point to the number one on the activity page. Explain that it is a picture of the tongue. When he eats food, he tastes it with his tongue. He chews the food into tiny pieces. Color the tongue red.

3. Ask him to point to the number two on the activity page. Explain that after he swallows the food, the food moves down the esophagus. Color the esophagus orange.

4. Ask your child to point to the number three on the activity page. Tell him number three is the stomach. The stomach breaks down food using acid. Color the stomach yellow.

5. Ask your child to point to the number four on the activity page. Tell him number four is the small intestines. The small intestines squeeze out all of the nutrients the body needs to stay strong and healthy and sends it into the body. Color all of the small intestines green.

6. Ask your preschooler to point to the number five on the activity page. Explain that number five is the large intestines. The parts of the food that are left over from the small intestines move into the large intestines. Color all of the large intestines blue.

7. Ask your preschooler to point to the number six on the activity page. Explain that number six is the rectum (or bottom). Whatever the body does not need from the food gets passed out of the body through poop. Color the rectum purple.

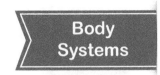

How Long is the Small Intestines?

Materials:

- ☐ Measuring Tape
- ☐ Garden Hose

Directions:

1. Tell your preschooler that his small intestines are about 20 feet long. Ask him if he would like to go outside and see an object that is as long as his intestines.

   **The average adult intestines ranges from 23-25 feet long, while a young child's small intestines is about 20 feet long. This varies between girls and boys and ages.

2. Show your child the garden hose. The garden hose is about the same diameter as the small intestines—one inch. Help your preschooler measure the diameter (distance of the opening of the hose) to see if it is one inch.

3. Now ask your preschooler to place the hose in as straight a line as possible.

4. Using the tape measure, ask him to place the end of the tape measure at the mouth of the hose and walk until he measures 20 feet.

5. Once he measures 20 feet of hose, remind him that all of the garden hose (small intestines) fits inside his tiny belly. Ask him if he can bunch up the 20 feet of garden hose small enough to fit in his belly.

LOW PREP *Taste Buds Collage*

Materials:

- ☐ Tongue Activity Page (Appendix AK)
- ☐ Crayons
- ☐ Scissors
- ☐ Glue
- ☐ Magazines

Directions:

1. Explain to your preschooler that his tongue has tiny bumps on it called taste buds. The taste buds are on different parts of his tongue to allow him to taste different foods. The taste buds tell his brain what he tastes.

2. Show your preschooler the *Tongue* activity page. Explain to your child that he will look through a magazine to find pictures of food, cut them out, and decide if it is bitter, sour, salty, or sweet.

   **If you do not have magazines, he can draw images of food in each section.

   **If your child is unsure what bitter, sour, salty, or sweet tastes like, allow him to sample a few items you have at home in each category.

3. As he is cutting out images of food, ask him which category he will glue the image onto. You can also ask him which types of foods he likes best.

Muscles

Make it Stronger

Directions:

1. Ask your preschooler to show you his muscles.

2. Explain to him that his body is full of muscles. He even has muscles in his face.

3. Ask your preschooler to find a specific muscle in his body (arm, shoulder, leg, back, fingers, cheeks, etc.). Now, ask him to show you an exercise that can make that muscle stronger.

You can provide him with examples of exercises if needed (push-ups for arms and shoulders, jumping jacks for legs, lay on his back and lifting legs up for abs, lay on his stomach and lift his arms and legs off the floor for back, etc.)

LOW PREP **Muscle Model**

Materials:

☐ Bendable Straw
☐ Ruler
☐ Scissors
☐ Tape
☐ Rubber Band
☐ ¼ inch 36" Wooden Dowel (Cut in Half)

Directions:

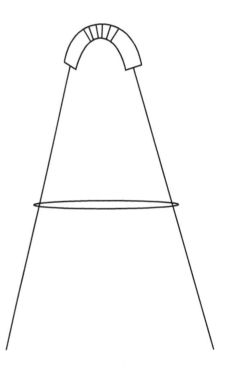

1. From the bendable portion of the straw, measure 2 inches out on either side of the bendable portion and cut the straw. You will use the bendable portion of the straw.

2. Ask your preschooler if he would like to make a model of a muscle. Ask him to insert one wooden dowel into the 2-inch portion of the straw.

3. Slide the other wooden dowel into the other 2-inch portion of the bendable straw.

4. Tape the straw closed around the wooden dowels, so the dowels will not fall out.

5. Ask your preschooler to slide a rubber band around both wooden dowels. It should be 6 inches from the bendable straw. It will look like a triangle after it is assembled.

6. Explain to your preschooler that the wooden dowels are like bones. They are strong and hard to move. The bendable straw is the joint between the bones—like the bend in his elbow or fingers. The rubber band is the muscle.

7. Ask your preschooler to pull the bones apart. Ask him what happens to the muscle. (It stretches or gets longer.)

8. Ask him to pull the bones close together. Ask him what happens to the muscle. (It gets shorter.)

9. Tell him that since bones can't move or bend, muscles have to do the work. Muscles are attached to bones.

Obstacle Course

Materials:

☐ Things Around the House

Directions:

1. Create an obstacle course for your child to use all of his muscles. This obstacle course can be outside or inside. Here are some ideas to include in your obstacle course:

    Climb through a tunnel

    Scooter to the next obstacle

    Climb over a piece of furniture

    Hop like a bunny to the next obstacle

    Kick a soccer ball on a straight line of chalk

    Pull a rope attached to a box filled with stuffed animals to the next obstacle

    Jump rope five times before heading to the next obstacle

    Use a toy hammer to hit five golf tees into the dirt

Nervous

Amazing Brain

Materials:

- ☐ Clear Container with Lid
- ☐ 2 Eggs
- ☐ Water

Directions:

1. Ask your preschooler if he would enjoy learning about his brain.

2. Ask him to place a raw egg inside a clear container and place the lid on it. Make sure the lid is on tight. Explain to your child the container represents his skull (the bone in his head) and the egg is his brain.

3. Now ask him to shake the container as hard as he can.
   What happens to the egg? (It probably broke.)

4. Clean out the container.

5. Ask your preschooler to place another raw egg inside the clear container.

6. Add enough water so that the egg is covered. Place the lid tightly on the container.

7. Explain that the container is still his skull, the egg is still his brain, and the water is the fluid that surrounds his brain called cerebrospinal fluid.

8. Ask your preschooler to shake the container as hard as he can. What happens to the egg? (It should stay intact.) Tell your child that the fluid around his brain helps protect his brain from getting hurt when he falls down.

Brain Hat

Materials:

- ☐ Brain Hat Activity Pages (Appendix AL)
- ☐ Crayons
- ☐ Scissors
- ☐ Stapler

Directions:

1. Ask your preschooler if he would enjoy making a brain hat.

2. Show him the *Brain Hat* activity pages. Explain that he will color the brain, and then together you will cut it out and staple the brain together to create a hat.

3. Tell your child there are different areas of the brain and each of those areas has a different job. Point to the frontal lobe. Explain that the frontal lobe helps him think, plan, organize, problem solve, and control his actions and emotions. It's his personality.

4. Point to the motor cortex. This part of the brain helps him move.

5. Point to the sensory cortex. This part of the brain helps him taste, smell, hear, and feel.

6. Point to the parietal lobe. This part of the brain helps him make sense of his experiences. The parietal lobe helps him learn to spell and do math.

7. Point to the occipital lobe. This part of the brain helps him to see and understand what he sees.

8. Point to the temporal lobe. This part of the brain holds memories. It also helps him learn how to speak.

9. Allow him to color the brain. He can color it as he pleases or color each lobe a different color.

10. Cut out the brain halves from the activity pages.

11. On the brain halves, there are dotted lines. Cut the dotted lines.

12. Now slide the dotted line over to the solid line and staple the two pieces together. Do this for each dotted line.

13. Now staple each brain half together to form the hat.

Memory Game

Materials:

☐ Folder
☐ Construction Paper

Directions:

1. Gather six different colors of construction paper. Cut eight 2-inch by 2-inch squares out of each color of construction paper.

2. Divide the squares evenly into two separate groups (same colors and same number in each group).

3. Ask your preschooler if he would like to test his brain.

4. Sit face to face in front of your child. Place the folder in between both of you as a divider.

5. Tell your preschooler that you will create a pattern using your colored squares on your side of the folder.

6. Next, remove the folder for five seconds so he can observe the pattern. After five seconds, place the folder back in front of the pattern you created, and ask your child to use his squares to do his best to create the same pattern on his side of the folder.

7. Start the game by creating the pattern using three colored squares. If your child is successful at creating the matching pattern then you can make a pattern using four colored squares the next round and so forth. However, if he struggles with making the pattern with three colored squares continue with the same number of colored squares until he can be successful.

Spine Model

Materials:

- ☐ 2 Pipe Cleaners
- ☐ Empty Egg Carton
- ☐ Cheerios, Fruit Loops, or Wagon Wheel Pasta

Directions:

1. First, cut the top half of the egg carton off. Now, cut apart each egg spot to have 12 little cups.

2. Poke a hole into one side of each egg carton cup. Poke a second hole in the side opposite of each egg carton cup.

3. Twist the two pipe cleaner ends together to form a long pipe cleaner.

4. Ask your preschooler if he would like to create a spine.

5. Ask him to thread the pipe cleaner through an egg carton cup.

6. Next, he will need to thread the pipe cleaners through a Cheerio.

7. Ask your child to continue this pattern until the pipe cleaner is full.

8. Twist the ends of the pipe cleaners so the pieces of the spine do not fall off.

9. Explain to your preschooler the different parts of the spine. The egg carton cups are the vertebrate—the bones that protect the spinal cord.

The Cheerios are the intervertebral discs that help the spine bend and move without the vertebrate rubbing together.

The pipe cleaner is the spinal cord. The spinal cord is very important. The spinal cord is the nerves that run from the brain to the body. This means that when his brain sees a cup and wants to pick it up, it sends a message down to the spinal cord. The spinal cord sends the message to his arm to tell his arm to pick up the cup.

The Ultimate Preschool Activity Guide | Autumn McKay

Skeleton

Bone Letters

Materials:

- ☐ Q-tips
- ☐ Scissors
- ☐ Paper
- ☐ Page Protector
- ☐ Dry Erase Marker
- ☐ Eraser

Directions:

1. Place a piece of paper inside a page protector. (If you have a small dry erase board you can use that.)

2. Using the dry erase marker, write a single letter on the dry erase board.

   **Focus on uppercase letters until your child is very familiar with each uppercase letter.

3. Cut six q-tips in half and leave six q-tips intact.

4. Invite your preschooler to make letters using bones. Explain to him that you will write a letter on the dry erase board, and he will use the bones (q-tips) to trace the letter by placing the bones along the lines of the letter.

5. As your preschooler creates the letter, ask him to identify the letter. Then ask him to tell you the sound of the letter.

6. Erase the letter and write a new letter for your child to trace with bones.

LOW PREP *Make a Skeleton*

Materials:

- ☐ Skeleton Activity Page (Appendix AM)
- ☐ Scissors
- ☐ Hole Puncher
- ☐ Brass Fasteners
- ☐ Crayons

Directions:

1. Ask your preschooler if he would like to create a skeleton. Show him the *Skeleton* activity page.

2. You can ask him to cut out each bone of the skeleton or you can cut out the bones.

3. Ask your preschooler to help hole punch each black dot on the bones.

4. Now ask him to help assemble the skeleton. Starting from the top, ask him to use a brass fastener to attach the skull and body.

5. From the shoulder, use a brass fastener to attach the shoulder and single bone. Attach another single bone with a brass fastener. There should be two single bones for each arm. Next, your preschooler can use a brass fastener to attach the hand to the arm bone.

6. Complete Step 5 for the other arm.

7. Ask your preschooler to attach a single bone to the skeleton's hip with a brass fastener. He can attach another single bone, and then the foot to the leg bone with the brass fastener. There should be two single bones for each leg.

8. Complete Step 7 for the other leg.

9. Now your child can draw a face on his skeleton.

Why are Bones Important?

Materials:

☐ Playdough
☐ Straw

Directions:

1. Tell your preschooler that bones are important and today he will do an experiment to discover why bones are important for his body.

2. Ask your child to use half of the playdough to create an arm without a bone.

3. Now ask him to use the other half of the playdough to create an arm with a bone. He will wrap the playdough around a straw (the bone) like a burrito.

4. Ask your child to stand each arm vertically onto the table.

5. Now ask him to use one hand to try to smash each arm by pressing down towards the table.

6. Ask him: which arm was easy to push down; what happened to each arm; why he thinks we have bones.

7. Tell your child that bones help people keep the same shape. Tell him that bones support a person's weight and allow people to stand upright, and walk and play.

Pancakes vs. Cookies

Materials:

- ☐ Gingerbread Man Shaped Pancake
- ☐ Gingerbread Man Shaped Cookie

Directions:

1. Make gingerbread shaped pancakes and cookies together with your child. Afterwards, talk about why bones and muscles are important. The cookie needs to be firm.

2. Explain to your preschooler that the pancake gingerbread man is like a body with only muscles. Ask him to feel it and move it. It is very bendable and doesn't stand up easily.

3. Now ask him to touch and feel the gingerbread man cookie. What does it feel like? This represents a body made of only bones. Does it move easily?

4. Bones are strong but don't bend easily. Ask him to try to bend the cookie. What happens? (It breaks.) Explain that this is why you need both muscles and bones. The muscles allow bones to move.

The Ultimate Preschool Activity Guide | Autumn McKay

Respiratory

Lung Craft

Materials:

- ☐ Lung Activity Page (Appendix AO)
- ☐ Red Tissue Paper
- ☐ Pink Tissue Paper
- ☐ Glue
- ☐ Crayons

Directions:

1. Cut out little squares of pink and red tissue paper.

2. Show your preschooler the *Lung* activity page. Explain to him that the lungs are located in his chest. He has two lungs to help him breathe. They are pink and squishy.

3. Tell your child that he will glue the pink and red tissue paper to the lungs. He can color the bronchus and trachea any color he wishes.

LOW PREP Lung Race

Materials:

- ☐ Cotton Balls

Directions:

1. Ask your preschooler if he would enjoy racing you. Explain that this will not be a normal race, but a race using his lungs.

2. Place a cotton ball at the edge of the table—one for each competitor.

3. Ask your child to blow the cotton ball across the table after you say, "Go."

4. The first competitor to blow the cotton ball off the other end of the table wins.

▶ LOW PREP ◀ *Measure Lung Capacity*

Materials:

☐ Balloon
☐ Flexible Tape Measure

Directions:

1. Ask your child if he would like to see the strength of his lungs.

   **I recommend your blowing up the balloon one time to allow the balloon to stretch out and making it easier for your preschooler to blow up.

2. Tell your child that he will use two breaths to blow up the balloon. Then he will hold the top of the balloon so the air does not come out of the balloon.

3. Use the tape measure to measure the diameter around the widest part of the balloon. This will be your preschooler's lung capacity (how much air his lungs hold).

4. Try this experiment a couple of times to see if he obtains different results. You can also try this to show him that each person's lungs hold a different amount of air.

LOW PREP *Paper Bag Lungs*

Materials:

☐ 2 Paper Lunch Bags
☐ 2 Straws
☐ Duct Tape
☐ Crayons (Optional)

Directions:

1. Ask your child if he would enjoy making lungs so he can see how lungs function.

2. Allow your child to use the crayons to color the paper bags if he desires.

3. Open up each paper bag.

4. Ask your preschooler to slide the straw into the bag about 3 inches.

5. Close the paper bag around the straw.

6. Tape the bag around the straw so no air can get into the bag, but don't squeeze the straw.

7. Follow Steps 3-6 for the other paper bag.

8. You can tape the straws together to represent the trachea.

9. Now ask your preschooler to place the straws in his mouth and blow into the bag. What happened? (The lungs (paper bags) should inflate.) Now ask him to breathe in. What happened to the lungs? (The lungs (paper bags) deflate.) Tell him this is what happens inside his own lungs each time he breathes.

Butterflies

Butterfly Addition

Materials:

- ☐ Piece of Paper
- ☐ Markers
- ☐ Pom Poms
- ☐ Die

Directions:

1. Draw a butterfly onto a piece of paper. Draw a plus sign on the body of the butterfly.

2. Invite your preschooler to create a butterfly with you.

3. Let him roll the die and count the dots.

4. Ask him to place the same number (from Step 3) of pom poms on the butterfly's left wing.

5. He will roll the die again and count the dots.

6. Your child will place the same number (from Step 5) of pom poms onto the butterfly's right wing.

7. Now ask him to add the pom pom from each wing together. He can count the total number of pom poms to discover the total.

8. State the math addition equation to your preschooler.

9. Repeat Steps 3-8 as many times as your preschooler would like.

LOW PREP *Caterpillar Patterns*

Materials:

- ☐ Piece of Paper
- ☐ Do-A-Dot Markers
- ☐ Marker

Directions:

1. Using the Do-A-Dot Markers create four separate patterns on a piece of paper. Form the patterns in a line to look like a caterpillar's body. Leave enough room for your child to continue the pattern. Example of patterns to create:

   Red, blue, red, blue, red, blue

   Green, orange, green, orange, green, orange, green

   Yellow, purple, purple, yellow, purple, purple, yellow

   Blue, red, green, blue, red, green, blue

   **If you do not have Do-A-Dot Markers, you can use a q-tip or a finger dipped in paint.

2. After the patterns are dry, use the marker to draw a face on each caterpillar.

3. Show your preschooler your caterpillar patterns. Explain to him that caterpillars eat lots of food to get bigger to turn into butterflies. Ask him to help you make the caterpillars bigger by adding to the patterns.

4. Show him the first pattern. Point to each color as you say the pattern.

5. Ask him which color comes next in the pattern. If he is confused, repeat the pattern back to him, but also ask him to say it with you.

6. Your child may use the Do-A-Dot Marker to complete the pattern and help the caterpillar grow bigger.

7. Complete each caterpillar pattern by following Steps 4-6.

The Ultimate Preschool Activity Guide | Autumn McKay

Coffee Filter Butterfly

Materials:

- ☐ 2 Coffee Filters
- ☐ Clothes Pin
- ☐ Pipe Cleaner (Cut in Half)
- ☐ Markers
- ☐ Small Bowl
- ☐ Water
- ☐ Eye Dropper
- ☐ Tray

Directions:

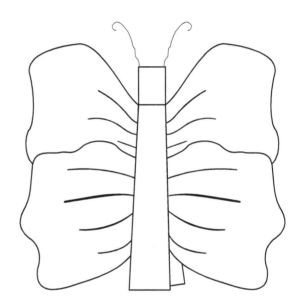

1. Ask your preschooler if he would like to create a butterfly.

2. Place two coffee filters in front of him. Ask him to use the markers to color each coffee filter anyway he pleases. (You might want to do this activity on a tray or piece of paper so the marker doesn't bleed through the filters.)

3. Place the small bowl of water and eye dropper in front of your child. Ask him to fill the eye dropper with water and squirt it over each coffee filter. He will want to cover each coffee filter with water.

4. Let the coffee filters dry.

5. After the coffee filters have dried, take one coffee filter and show your preschooler how to fold it like an accordion (back and forth). Ask him to do the same with the other coffee filter.

6. Pinch the clothes pin to open it. Place each folded coffee filter in between the clothes pin. Allow the clothes pin to close. While the filters are in the clothes pin, unfold the filters to create the wings.

7. Now, fold the cut pipe cleaner to form a V-shape. This is the antennae. Place the antennae in between the clothes pin just like the coffee filters.

LOW PREP *How to Draw a Butterfly*

Materials:

☐ Butterfly Drawing Activity Page (Appendix AP)
☐ Pencil
☐ Crayons

Directions:

1. Show your child the *Butterfly Drawing* activity page. Explain that he will follow the steps to draw his own butterfly.

2. Tell your child he is to only draw a small part on each step. Each new part he needs to add to his butterfly will be in red.

3. Ask him what he needs to draw in Step 1 on the activity page. Let him draw it.

4. Let him continue through each step by himself (if he can). This will help him learn to follow directions and build confidence in his independence.

5. He can color his butterfly after he draws it.

LOW PREP *Noodle Life Cycle*

Materials:

☐ Butterfly Life Cycle Activity Page (Appendix AQ)
☐ Glue
☐ Small Shell Pasta
☐ Regular Shell Pasta
☐ Rotini Pasta
☐ Farfalle Pasta

Directions:

1. Tell your preschooler that butterflies don't start out as butterflies—they begin as tiny eggs. Ask him if he wants you to show him how eggs turn into butterflies.

2. Show your child the *Butterfly Life Cycle* activity page.

3. Explain to your child that butterflies start as eggs. Show him the small shell pasta. Ask him to glue three or four small shell pasta onto the leaf to look like eggs.

4. Tell him when the eggs hatch, a caterpillar comes out from the egg. Show your preschooler the rotini pasta. Ask him to glue the rotini pasta in the grass. Explain that the caterpillar has to eat a lot of grass and leaves to grow and grow.

5. Tell your preschooler when the caterpillar is big enough, it will find a safe place to build a cocoon or chrysalis. Show your preschooler the regular shell pasta. Ask him to glue the cocoon onto the tree branch.

6. Explain to your child that in approximately 14 days, the cocoon starts to hatch and out comes a butterfly. Show your preschooler the farfalle pasta. Let him glue the butterfly pasta onto the cloud picture.

7. Ask your child if he can tell you the life cycle of the butterfly using his picture.

Pollen Transfer

Materials:

- ☐ Construction Paper
- ☐ Scissors
- ☐ Pipe Cleaner
- ☐ Powdered Cheese from Macaroni and Cheese Box

Directions:

1. Cut out one big flower from construction paper, as well as, five or six small flowers.

2. Pour a medium amount of the powdered cheese into the middle of the large flower.

3. Ask your preschooler if he would enjoy being a butterfly and investigating how butterflies move pollen.

4. Cut a pipe cleaner in half. Take one half and wrap it one time around your child's index (at the middle knuckle). Let the loose ends of the pipe cleaner hang on the underside of his finger. Make a slight bend on the ends to form the butterfly feet.

5. Take the other half of the pipe cleaner. Wrap it one time around your child's index finger (at the fingernail). Let the loose ends of the pipe cleaner point upwards on the top side of his finger. Twirl the ends downward to form butterfly antennae.

6. Ask your child to fly his butterfly around to the flowers. As he is flying the butterfly around, ask him to land in the pollen of the large flower and then fly to drink the nectar of another flower.

7. Ask your preschooler to inspect what happened after he flew from the large flower to the smaller flower. What is on the butterfly's legs? What is on the smaller flower? Did any pollen fall while he was flying to the flower?

8. Explain that moving pollen from one plant to the next helps the plants grow, so the butterflies are helping plants grow.

LOW PREP *Very Hungry Caterpillar Sequence*

Materials:

☐ Very Hungry Caterpillar Activity Page (Appendix AR)
☐ *The Very Hungry Caterpillar* by Eric Carle
☐ Crayons
☐ Scissors
☐ Single Hole Puncher

Directions:

1. Show your preschooler the *Very Hungry Caterpillar* activity page. Ask him to color the pictures.

2. Read *The Very Hungry Caterpillar* by Eric Carle to your child, but as you are reading stop after each day in the story.

3. Ask your child what the caterpillar ate. Then ask him to use the hole puncher to eat through (punch a hole) the food the caterpillar just ate.

4. Continue with the story, stopping after each day so your child can recall what food the caterpillar has already eaten and just ate.

Construction

LOW PREP *Add Nuts and Bolts*

Materials:

☐ Nuts and Bolts Activity Page (Appendix AS)
☐ Bolts
☐ Nuts

Directions:

1. Ask your preschooler to join you as you add nuts and bolts together. Show him the *Nuts and Bolts* activity page.

2. Show him the first ten frame on the activity page. Point to the number of bolts needed to place in the ten frame (4).

3. Ask your child to place four bolts inside the ten frame—each box receiving only one bolt.

4. Now point to the number of nuts needed to place in the ten frame (6).

5. Ask your child to place six nuts inside the remaining boxes of the ten frame.

6. Ask your preschooler to count the total number of nuts and bolts in the ten frame.

7. Say the math problem to him (4 + 6 = 10).

8. Repeat Steps 2-7 for the other ten frames on the activity page.

LOW PREP *Build Letters with Rocks*

Materials:

☐ Page Protector ☐ Dry Erase Marker
☐ Piece of Paper ☐ Small Pebbles

Directions:

1. Ask your preschooler if he would enjoy using rocks to create letters.

    **I found bags of small pebble rocks at the Dollar Store.

2. Place the paper inside the page protector.

3. Use the dry erase marker to write a letter onto the page protector.

    **Write uppercase letters if your child is still learning letter recognition.

4. Now ask your child to trace the letter by placing the pebble rocks along the lines of the letter.

5. When he is finished, ask him to identify the letter and letter sound.

6. Erase the letter and complete Steps 3-5 with another letter.

▶ LOW PREP ◀ *Count and Wreck*

Materials:

☐ Building Blocks
☐ Construction Trucks (Optional)

Directions:

1. Ask your preschooler if he would enjoy destroying towers.

2. Gather your child's construction trucks and building blocks. If he doesn't have construction trucks, that's not a problem.

3. Tell your preschooler you will call out a number and he will build a tower with said number of blocks.

4. Call out a number, and allow him to build his tower.

5. Now for the fun part, ask him to use his construction trucks or fist to knock the tower down.

6. Complete Steps 4 and 5 as many times as he enjoys.

LOW PREP *Hammer Syllables*

Materials:

☐ Hammer Syllables Activity Page (Appendix AT)
☐ Toy Hammer (Optional)
☐ Unifix Cubes (Optional)

Directions:

1. Ask your preschooler if he could help you hammer.

2. Show your preschooler the *Hammer Syllables* activity page.

3. Point to the first image on the activity page. Ask him to tell you the name of the image.

4. Ask him to use his hammer to tap out the syllables of the word. For example, "hammer" would be "ham-mer," so two taps.

5. For each word, ask your preschooler how many syllables are in the word. Then, to tap the number at the bottom of the activity page.

6. If your preschooler would enjoy it, tell him to place the same number of Unifix cubes on each image as the number of syllables to help him visualize the number of syllables in each word.

Measuring

Materials:

- ☐ Something with Which to Measure (Tape Measure, Unifix Cubes, etc.)
- ☐ Painter's Tape

Directions:

1. Explain to your preschooler that construction workers have to measure building materials (e.g., wood, water pipes, wiring) to build things correctly. Ask him if he would like to learn how to measure like a construction worker.

    **If your preschooler has never seen or used a tape measure before, I recommend learning how to measure with Unifix cubes or blocks first.

2. Place varying lengths of tape across the table, floor, or piece of paper.

3. Ask your child to measure each piece of tape with the Unifix cubes or blocks.

4. If your preschooler is proficient in number recognition, then introduce the tape measure to him and allow him to measure the pieces of tape using a tape measure.

LOW PREP ## Play with Nuts, Bolts, and Washers

Materials:

- ☐ Nuts
- ☐ Bolts
- ☐ Washers

Directions:

Gather nuts, bolts, and washers and allow your child to build as he pleases. He can twist the nuts onto the bolts, slide washers onto a bolt and then twist a nut on the bolt, or any other action that allows him to connect them together.

This activity gives your child a fun way to develop the fine motor skills he needs to be able to grasp a pencil correctly.

LOW PREP *Sort Pom Poms*

Materials:

☐ Assortment of Colored Pom Poms
☐ Construction Trucks

Directions:

1. Spread out an assortment of colored pom poms on the floor. Explain to your preschooler that the construction workers need help sorting all of the pom poms into groups of colors.

2. Allow your child to use the construction trucks to push, carry, and dump pom poms into different color groups.

3. Allow your preschooler to do this activity as many times as he pleases.

LOW PREP *What Can You Create?*

Materials:

☐ Assortment of Legos
☐ Cup

Directions:

1. Place an assortment of Legos into a cup.

2. Show your preschooler the cup of Legos. Ask him to look at the cup of Legos and decide what he could create and build with only the Legos provided in the cup.

This allows your child to build his imagination, creativity, and problem-solving skills.

Cooking

LOW PREP *Applesauce*

Materials:

- ☐ 5 lbs Apples
- ☐ 1 ½ Cup of Water
- ☐ 1 Tablespoon Cinnamon
- ☐ 2 Tablespoons Sugar (Optional)

- ☐ Pot
- ☐ Blender or Hand Blender
- ☐ Knife
- ☐ Plastic Knife

Directions:

1. Wash your and your preschooler's hands before beginning.

2. Peel and core each apple.

3. Place the apples on a paper plate and allow your preschooler to use a plastic knife to slice the apples. (If the use of a plastic knife is not appropriate for your child, please do this for him.)

4. Ask your preschooler to place all apple slices into the pot.

5. Ask him to pour the water, cinnamon, and sugar (only if you want sweetened applesauce) into the pot.

6. Let the apples cook in the pot with the lid on for 20-30 minutes or until very soft to touch with a fork.

7. Pour the apple mixture into a blender and blend until smooth. You may also use a hand blender in the pot to create smooth applesauce.

8. Enjoy the delicious treat once it is cool to the touch.

LOW PREP *Banana Split Pudding*

Materials:

☐ Chocolate Pudding (Prepared From Mix or Pudding Cups)
☐ Vanilla Pudding (Prepared From Mix or Pudding Cups)
☐ Whipped Cream
☐ Banana
☐ Strawberries
☐ Crushed Pineapple
☐ Sprinkles
☐ Cups
☐ Plastic Knife
☐ Plastic Drinking Straw

Directions:

1. Invite your preschooler to help prepare dessert for the family. Wash hands.

2. If you purchased the pudding mix, ask your preschooler to help prepare the pudding so that is ready when needed.

3. Wash the strawberries. Ask your child to remove the leaves and tops of the strawberries by pushing the plastic straw through the bottom of the strawberry to the top. This will help the leaves pop right off.

4. Ask him to use his plastic knife to cut the strawberries into bite size pieces. (If the use of a plastic knife is not appropriate for your child, please do this for him.)

5. Now, peel the banana. Ask your preschooler to use his plastic knife to slice the banana.

6. Drain the crushed pineapple. You might want to do this step to help your child avoid sharp edges on the can.

7. It is now time to assemble the banana splits! Ask your preschooler to place the sliced bananas on the bottom of each cup, then scoop chocolate pudding on top of the bananas, add strawberries, scoop vanilla pudding into each cup, add crushed pineapple, top with whipped cream and sprinkles.

8. Enjoy!

Chocolate Bark

Materials:

- ☐ 10 oz Dark Chocolate
- ☐ 1 Cup Macadamia Nuts
- ☐ ½ Teaspoon Sea Salt
- ☐ Wax Paper
- ☐ Cookie Sheet
- ☐ Glass Bowl
- ☐ Knife
- ☐ Spoon

Directions:

1. Ask your preschooler if he would like to make a special treat.

2. Be sure to wash hands before beginning.

3. The parent will need to roughly chop the Macadamia nuts to prevent any harm to your child with a sharp knife.

4. Ask your preschooler to pour the chocolate into a glass bowl.

5. Place the bowl in the microwave heating it in 30 second increments. Allow your child to stir in between heating sessions until melted.

6. Once the chocolate is completely melted, ask your child to pour in the chopped nuts and stir.

7. Spread wax paper across a cookie sheet, and then pour the chocolate mixture onto the wax paper.

8. Ask your preschooler to spread the mixture across the wax paper evenly.

9. Sprinkle with Sea Salt.

10. Place the cookie sheet in the refrigerator for at least 30 minutes or until the chocolate is solid.

11. Once solid, you can have your preschooler break the bark into pieces and enjoy.

12. Store the bark at room temperature.

LOW PREP *Pizza*

Materials:

- ☐ Tortillas
- ☐ Pizza Sauce
- ☐ Pizza Toppings
- ☐ Cookie Sheet
- ☐ Spoon

Directions:

1. Ask your preschooler if he would enjoy making pizza. Be sure to wash hands before cooking.

2. Preheat the oven to 375°F.

3. Place tortillas onto a cookie sheet.

4. Ask him to use a spoon to scoop pizza sauce onto each tortilla. He can use the back of the spoon to spread the sauce around the tortilla.

5. Allow him to add cheese over the pizza sauce and his desired toppings (pepperoni, sausage, ham, pineapple, peppers, etc.).

6. When he has finished placing the toppings on his pizzas, place the cookie sheet in the oven for 10-12 minutes.

7. Allow the pizzas to cool before cutting them into slices and eating.

LOW PREP *Popcorn on the Cob*

Materials:

- ☐ Dried Corn on the Cob
- ☐ Paper Lunch Bag
- ☐ Microwave

Directions:

1. Ask your preschooler what he thinks would happen if he put a dried corn cob in the microwave.

2. Let him place the corn cob inside the paper bag.

3. Fold the top of the bag over a couple of times so the steam doesn't escape the bag.

4. Place the bag in the microwave.

5. Set the microwave to popcorn setting (or 2 ½ minutes).

6. Let your child listen for the sound of popping.

7. When the microwave turns off, open the bag and let your preschooler see what happened to the corn on the cob.

8. Let him enjoy a snack.

LOW PREP *Rainbow Milk Toast*

Materials:

- ☐ Bread Slices
- ☐ Milk
- ☐ Food Coloring
- ☐ Clean Paintbrushes
- ☐ Toaster
- ☐ Small Bowls

Directions:

1. Ask your preschooler if he would enjoy painting his food.

2. Be sure to wash hands before beginning.

3. In a few small bowls, mix together one to two tablespoons of milk and food coloring. Allow your child to pick the colors.

   **The more fat in the milk the brighter the colors tend to be on the bread.

4. Place a piece of bread on a plate and allow your preschooler to use the paintbrushes to create a picture on his bread.

5. Once complete, place the bread in the toaster.

6. Let cool. Let him enjoy his edible art.

LOW PREP *Sausage Balls*

Materials:

- ☐ 1 ¼ Cups of Flour
- ☐ 1 ½ Teaspoon of Baking Powder
- ☐ ½ Teaspoon of Salt
- ☐ ¼ Teaspoon of Black Pepper
- ☐ ½ Teaspoon of Ground Cayenne Pepper
- ☐ ½ Teaspoon of Garlic Powder
- ☐ ½ Teaspoon of Onion Powder
- ☐ 8oz Shredded Sharp Cheddar Cheese
- ☐ 1lb Breakfast Sausage
- ☐ 8oz Cream Cheese
- ☐ Mixing Bowl or Standing Mixer
- ☐ Cookie Sheet

Directions:

1. Ask your preschooler if he would enjoy helping you make breakfast.

2. Wash hands before cooking.

3. Preheat the oven to 400°F.

4. Ask your preschooler to help you pour all of the dry ingredients into the mixing bowl. Stir together.

5. Allow him to add the shredded cheddar cheese. Stir together.

6. Now ask him to add in the cream cheese. Mix together.

7. Add in the sausage. Mix together until all combined.

8. Scoop the mixture into about 32 equal size balls onto the cookie sheet. Place about 1-inch apart.

9. Bake in oven for 18-20 minutes.

10. When finished, allow the sausage balls to cool for a few minutes before enjoying.

LOW PREP Sensory Measuring

Materials:

- ☐ Rice
- ☐ Measuring Cups
- ☐ Measuring Spoons
- ☐ Bowls

Directions:

1. Pour the rice into a bowl. Place measuring spoons and measuring cups around the bowl.

2. Invite your preschooler to play with the objects.

3. He can measure different amounts, see how many cups it takes to fill another bowl, or compare how much a measuring cup and measuring spoon hold.

LOW PREP Smoothie

Materials:

- ☐ Blender
- ☐ Cups
- ☐ Frozen Fruit of Choice
- ☐ Fresh Fruit of Choice
- ☐ Vegetables of Choice
- ☐ Milk
- ☐ Protein (Optional)

Directions:

1. Ask your preschooler if he would like to help you make a yummy smoothie for everyone.

   **I will share our favorite smoothie recipe for a family of five: 3 cups milk, 1 fresh banana, 1 stalk of kale, another fresh vegetable (carrot, spinach, cauliflower, 1/8 beet, or avocado), frozen strawberries, 2 scoops whey protein

2. Ask your preschooler to place each ingredient inside the blender.

3. Place the top on the blender and allow him to be in control of the buttons. Blend until smooth.

4. Once smooth, pour into the cups and enjoy!

Sprinkle Counting

Materials:

- ☐ Playdough
- ☐ 12 Cupcake Liners
- ☐ 12 Index Cards
- ☐ Muffin Pan
- ☐ Marker
- ☐ Play Sprinkles (Little Buttons, Cut Up Pipe Cleaners, Pom Poms, etc.)

Directions:

1. Using the index cards, make numbered flash cards for numbers 1-12. Mix the cards up.

2. Place the cupcake liners inside the muffin pan.

3. Use the playdough to make 12 medium balls. Place each ball inside the cupcake liner to be a pretend cupcake.

4. Invite your preschooler to help you decorate the pretend cupcakes.

5. Ask your preschooler to flip over an index card and read the number.

6. He will then place the number of play sprinkles from Step 5 on top of the playdough cupcake.

7. Repeat Steps 5 and 6 until all cupcakes are decorated.

Dinosaurs

Build a Dinosaur

Materials:

- ☐ Build a Dinosaur Activity Page (Appendix AU)
- ☐ Playdough
- ☐ Scissors
- ☐ Page Protectors or Laminator (Optional)

Directions:

1. I recommend cutting apart each dinosaur image on the *Build a Dinosaur* activity pages and placing them inside a page protector or laminating them. This will allow your preschooler to use the activity pages multiple times.

2. Invite your child to come build dinosaurs with playdough.

3. Let him pick an image of a dinosaur from the activity pages.

4. Tell him the name of the dinosaur.

5. Allow him to manipulate the playdough to create the correct shapes to form the outline of the dinosaur image.

6. Complete Steps 3-5 for each dinosaur.

LOW PREP ## Catch the Dinosaur

Materials:

- ☐ Wide Jar with Lid
- ☐ Plastic Easter Egg
- ☐ Small Plastic Dinosaur
- ☐ Water

Directions:

1. Place the larger half of the plastic Easter egg inside the jar along with the small plastic dinosaur (the dinosaur should be able to fit inside the egg half).

2. Fill the jar with water and screw the lid on tight.

3. Ask your preschooler if he can move the jar around to catch the dinosaur inside the egg.

The Ultimate Preschool Activity Guide | Autumn McKay

LOW PREP *Dinosaur Fossils*

Materials:

- ☐ 2 Cups of Flour
- ☐ 1 Cup of Salt
- ☐ 1 Cup of Water
- ☐ Mixing Bowl
- ☐ Cookie Sheet
- ☐ Paint
- ☐ Paintbrushes
- ☐ Plastic Dinosaurs (Optional)

Directions:

1. Ask your preschooler if he would like to make dinosaur fossils. Explain that when dinosaurs died their bodies were covered with dirt, mud, and sand. The soft part of the dinosaur, the skin, goes away over time, but the harder parts like bones and teeth remain. The mud presses down on the bones over a long time and makes a hard fossil.

2. Preheat the oven to 325°F.

3. Allow your child to mix the flour, salt and water in the mixing bowl.

4. Knead the dough until firm.

5. Roll the dough out and flatten it.

6. Allow your preschooler to press the plastic dinosaur toys into the dough to form an imprint of the dinosaur. If you do not have plastic dinosaurs, you can use leaves, other toys, or even form the dough to make bone-like shapes.

7. After the fossils have been made, place them on a cookie sheet.

8. Bake the fossils for 30 minutes per inch of thickness (Ex. A fossil that is 2 inches thick needs to bake for 60 minutes.)

9. Allow the fossils to cool completely.

10. Your child can now paint his fossils if he pleases.

Dinosaur Name

Materials:

- ☐ Dinosaur Name Activity Pages (Appendix AV)
- ☐ Crayons
- ☐ Scissors

Directions:

1. Write each letter of your child's name on the dinosaur spikes on the second *Dinosaur Name* activity page.

   **Use uppercase letters if your child is just beginning to learn letter recognition.

2. Cut out the spikes that you wrote letters on.

3. Allow your preschooler to color the dinosaur and cut-out spikes.

4. Ask your preschooler if he can help the dinosaur put his spikes back in place. In order to get all the spikes back in the right place, he will need to use the spikes to spell his name.

5. Help direct your child with picking the correct letter that comes next in his name.

6. When he has his name spelled, point to each letter as you say it. Now, slide your finger under the word as you read his name to him. Ask your child to spell his name.

LOW PREP *Dinosaur Puppets*

Materials:

☐ Dinosaur Puppet Activity Page (Appendix AW)
☐ Crayons
☐ Scissors
☐ Clothes Pins
☐ Glue

Directions:

1. Ask your preschooler if he would like to make chomping dinosaurs.

2. Show him the *Dinosaur Puppet* activity page.

3. Ask him to color each dinosaur.

4. Either of you can cut out each dinosaur. You will also need to cut along the dotted line across the mouth of each dinosaur.

5. Now, lay the clothes pin on its side. Glue the top half of the dinosaur to the edge of the top of the clothes pin.

6. Glue the bottom half of the dinosaur to the edge of the bottom of the clothes pin.

7. Complete Steps 5 and 6 for each dinosaur.

8. Allow your child to play with each chomping dinosaur.

Dinosaur Sort

Materials:

☐ Dinosaur Bones Activity Page (Appendix AX)
☐ Scissors

Directions:

1. Cut out each bone on the *Dinosaur Bones* activity page.

2. Mix the bones up.

3. Explain to your preschooler that dinosaurs have a lot of bones that are different sizes. All of these bones together make the dinosaur big and strong. Tell him you have a lot of pretend dinosaur bones that you need help sorting.

4. Lay the dinosaur bones in front of your child, in no particular order.

5. Ask him to sort the bones in order from smallest to biggest.

6. You can mix the bones up again and ask him to sort from biggest to smallest.

Rescue the Dinosaurs

Materials:

☐ Toy Dinosaurs
☐ Large Bowl
☐ Salt
☐ Spoons
☐ Eye Droppers
☐ Baster
☐ Paintbrushes
☐ Squirt Bottle
☐ Water
☐ Small Bowls

Directions:

I recommend this activity be done outside, in the bathtub, or in a shallow storage container.

1. Begin by filling the large bowl with water. Place the toy dinosaurs inside the water. You may find other items to include in the water, such as leaves, rocks, or twigs.

2. Place the bowl of items in the freezer. Allow the water to freeze until completely frozen.

3. Once frozen, run a bit of warm water around the edge of the bowl to help the iced dinosaurs release from the bowl.

4. Place the frozen dinosaurs outside and invite your child to rescue the dinosaurs from the ice.

5. Provide him with tools to help him rescue the dinosaurs, like a bowl of salt, a bowl of warm water, eye droppers, spoons, paintbrushes, baster, squirt bottle, etc. Let him discover the best way to save the dinosaurs from their frozen captivity.

Engineer

LOW PREP *House Building*

Materials:

☐ *The Three Little Pigs* book
☐ Playdough
☐ Q-tips
☐ Popsicle Sticks
☐ Straws
☐ Tissue Paper
☐ Other Craft Supplies Available

Directions:

1. Read *The Three Little Pigs* book with your preschooler.

2. Discuss with your preschooler how each house in the story was made of different materials. Talk about why the brick house was stronger than the straw house, and then ask your preschooler if he could build a house the big bad wolf could not blow down.

3. Lay out all of the supplies (You may choose any supplies you have at your home. You are not limited to the above items.). Ask your child to create a house using these items that can keep a pig safe when the big bad wolf comes to blow it down.

4. You will probably be surprised what your child constructs. When he is finished, pretend to be the big bad wolf and attempt to blow the house down.

5. If you do blow it down, ask your preschooler if he can think of a way to make the house stronger. This will help teach him to problem-solve.

6. After he has strengthened his house, you can be the big bad wolf again. Hopefully his house is strong enough, but if not, he can work on making it stronger again.

LOW PREP *Magic Stars*

Materials:

- ☐ Toothpicks
- ☐ Plate
- ☐ Eye Dropper
- ☐ Water

Directions:

1. Ask your preschooler if he knew stars were magic. Invite him to join you to see the magic star.

2. Carefully bend each toothpick in half until they snap, but are not broken completely apart. It might take a couple of attempts to get this right.

3. Arrange the toothpicks on the plate with the middles (the bent part) of each toothpick touching to form a closed star shape.

4. Ask your preschooler to fill the eye dropper with water.

5. He can then slowly add a few drops of water to the center of the star.

6. Wait and see what happens.

7. You can explain to your child the toothpicks are made of dried wood. When the toothpicks were bent in half, some parts of the wood stretch out and other parts became compressed inside the toothpick. All of the bent parts of the toothpicks were placed together, then water was added to the bent part. The bent part absorbed the water and became swollen. As the wood swelled it caused the toothpicks to straighten. As each toothpick straightened, the pointy ends of the toothpicks pushed against each other causing the star to open.

LOW PREP *Make a Bouncy Ball*

Materials:

- ☐ 1 Tablespoon of Borax
- ☐ ½ Cup of Warm Water
- ☐ 2 Tablespoons of White Elmer's Glue
- ☐ 1 Tablespoon of Cornstarch
- ☐ Food Coloring (Optional)

- ☐ Small Bowls
- ☐ Measuring Cups
- ☐ Spoon
- ☐ Fork

Directions:

1. Ask your preschooler if he would enjoy making a bouncy ball.

2. Ask your preschooler to help measure the warm water and Borax. Pour into a bowl.

3. Ask him to stir the mixture until the Borax is dissolved.

4. In a separate bowl, combine the glue and cornstarch. You may add food coloring to this mixture if desired. Stir.

5. Have your preschooler pour the glue mixture into the Borax water. Let it sit for 10-15 seconds. The glue mixture should begin to harden.

6. Pull out the glue mixture with a fork.

7. Ask your preschooler to begin to roll the glue mixture blob between his hands to form a ball. (If the ball still feels sticky, dip it back in the Borax water to firm it up.)

8. Once the ball is formed, allow your preschooler to try bouncing it.

9. If you plan to keep the ball, store it in an airtight container or it will dry out.

10. Explain to your child that when he added the glue to the Borax water the glue became firm and bouncy because the Borax reacted with the glue causing molecules in the glue to stick together.

    Think about cooked spaghetti. When freshly cooked spaghetti is strained, the pasta strands flow like a liquid slipping all over one another. A few minutes after the water has drained off, the pasta and the strands of spaghetti start to stick to each other a little. If the pasta is left even longer, the spaghetti strands really stick together and the spaghetti becomes one rubbery chunk. The same thing happens when making the bouncy ball.

LOW PREP *Make a Harmonica*

Materials:

- ☐ 2 Craft Sticks
- ☐ Wide Rubber Band (#64 Size)
- ☐ Plastic Drinking Straw
- ☐ 2 Small Rubber Bands
- ☐ Ruler
- ☐ Scissors

Directions:

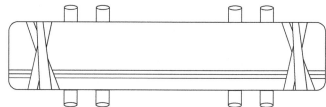

1. Ask your preschooler if he would enjoy making a harmonica. Explain that a harmonica is a musical instrument.

2. Ask your preschooler to stretch the wide rubber band around the length of one craft stick.

3. Use the scissors to cut four pieces of straw. Each piece needs to measure 1 ½ inches long.

4. Use the ruler to measure 2 inches from the left side of the craft stick. Place a piece of straw under the rubber band perpendicular to the craft stick. This is Straw 1.

5. Ask your preschooler to place another piece of straw on top of the rubber band to the right of Straw 1. This is Straw 2.

6. Use the ruler to measure 2 inches from the right side of the craft stick. Place a piece of straw under the rubber band perpendicular to the craft stick. This is Straw 3.

7. Place the last straw piece to the right of Straw 3 on top of the rubber band. This is Straw 4.

8. Hold the straws in place and ask your child to place the second craft stick on top of the first one. This will create a sandwich with the straws between the two craft sticks.

9. Secure the craft sticks by wrapping the small rubber bands around the ends of the two craft sticks.

10. Your child can adjust the straw placement by sliding them back and forth between the craft sticks.

11. Ask him to gently hold the instrument like a sandwich by holding each end of the craft sticks. Try to keep fingers close to the rubber bands on the end.

12. Ask your child to blow through the opening between the craft sticks. Do not blow through the straws. The rubber band in the middle of the two craft sticks needs to vibrate to make a sound.

LOW PREP *Playdough Marble Race Track*

Materials:

- ☐ Cookie Sheet
- ☐ Playdough
- ☐ Marble

Directions:

1. Invite your preschooler to help you make a race track for a marble.

2. Prop up a cookie sheet using a couple of building blocks or books. This will make it easier for the marble to roll from the top of the cookie sheet to the bottom.

3. Ask your preschooler to help you roll "snakes" in the playdough. These can be varying lengths.

4. Place the "snakes" onto the cookie sheet to create a race track for the marble to follow. Press the playdough into place.

5. Allow your preschooler to test out how the marble rolls down the cookie sheet with each "snake" placement so he can decide where to place the next "snake."

6. Once he has his race track complete, allow him to test it.

7. If he would like to do the activity again, allow him to make the race track without any help.

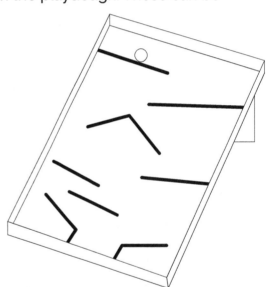

LOW PREP *Which Shape is Strongest?*

Materials:

☐ 3 Sheets of Paper
☐ Tape
☐ Books

Directions:

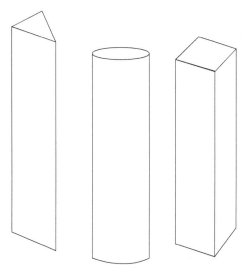

1. Explain to your preschooler that you want to see if paper is strong enough to hold a stack of books.

2. Invite your preschooler to help make shape tubes out of the paper.

3. Roll up one sheet of paper to make a cylinder. Tape the ends in place.

4. Fold another piece of paper into three equal columns. Form the folds together to make a triangular prism. Tape the ends in place.

5. Fold the last piece of paper into four equal columns. Form the folds together to make a rectangular prism. Tape the ends in place.

6. Stand each paper shape vertically on a flat surface.

7. Ask your preschooler to gather some books.

8. Ask him to place one book at a time on top of the rectangular prism. Count how many books it can hold until it collapses.

9. Now, ask him to place one book at a time on top of the triangular prism. Count how many books it can hold until it collapses. Which tower held more books?

10. Lastly, ask your child to place one book at a time on top of the cylinder. Count how many books it can hold until it collapses. Which tower held the most books?

11. It's likely the cylinder held the most books. Explain to your child that because the cylinder didn't have edges, the weight of the books is evenly divided around the whole shape.

Family

LOW PREP *Dotted Family Names*

Materials:

- ☐ Paper
- ☐ Marker
- ☐ Do-A-Dot Markers

Directions:

**If you do not have Do-A-Dot Markers, use paint and Q-tips instead.

1. Write each family members name that lives in your home on a piece of paper in large letters.

2. Invite your preschooler to learn about his family. Show him each person's name. Read the names together. Ask him if any of the family members have the same letters in their names as his name.

3. Ask him to pick a name. Instruct him to use a Do-A-Dot Marker to trace each letter of the name.

4. Repeat Step 4 for each family member's name.

5. After your child has finished this activity, he may enjoy cutting the names out and giving each family member his or her name as a gift.

Family Match

Materials:

☐ Family Match Activity Page (Appendix AY)
☐ Scissors

Directions:

1. Cut out each family member card on the *Family Match* activity pages.

2. Shuffle the cards.

3. Lay them in a grid, face down.

4. Invite your preschooler to play a game with you.

5. Explain that each card has a match to it. He must flip over two cards on his turn. If the cards are the same family member he gets to keep the cards, but if the cards are two different family members, he will need to turn the cards back over and wait until his next turn.

6. The person with the most matching cards at the end of the game wins.

Family Scavenger Hunt

Materials:

☐ Family Scavenger Hunt Activity Page (Appendix AZ)
☐ Scissors

Directions:

1. Use the premade clues on the *Family Scavenger Hunt* activity page or create your own clues using the blank cards on the second Family Scavenger Hunt activity page. Cut out the cards you will be using.

2. Here are the answers to the clues:

   1. Kitchen table chair

   2. Toothbrush

   3. Toy box

   4. Closet or Shoe Holder

   5. Refrigerator

   6. Bed

   7. Tub

3. Work backwards placing the clues. Clue 8 will be placed in the tub. Clue 7 will be placed in the bed. Clue 6 will be placed in the refrigerator. Clue 5 will be placed in the closet. Clue 4 will be placed in the toy box. Clue 3 will be placed by a toothbrush. Clue 2 will be placed under a kitchen chair. You will hand your child Clue 1.

4. You can place a prize in the tub with Clue 8 if you wish.

5. Ask your entire family to participate in the scavenger hunt.

6. Hand the first clue to your child. Read the clue together with your child.

7. Ask your family to decide what the answer might be, and then go to the location as a family.

8. Congratulate everyone when the scavenger hunt is complete.

LOW PREP *Tube Family*

Materials:

- ☐ Toilet Paper Tube for Each Family Member
- ☐ Paint
- ☐ Paintbrushes
- ☐ Googly Eyes
- ☐ Yarn
- ☐ Scissors
- ☐ Glue
- ☐ Black Marker

Directions:

1. Ask your preschooler if he would enjoy making little family members.

2. Present him with a toilet paper tube for each family member that lives in your home. Cut the toilet paper tube down to size to represent the members' heights.

3. Draw a line around the top portion of the tube to separate the head from the body.

4. Allow your child to paint each family member's head skin color and choose a paint color to paint the clothes on the tube's body.

5. Allow the tubes to dry.

6. Let your preschooler choose a yarn color for each tube family member. Cut the yarn into pieces that suit the length of each family member.

7. Glue the hair to the top of the correct tube family member.

8. Glue the googly eyes to each tube family member's face.

9. Draw a mouth with the marker.

10. Your child will enjoy playing with the family members when finished.

LOW PREP *Who Lives in Your House?*

Materials:

☐ House Activity Page (Appendix BA)
☐ Crayons
☐ Pencil

Directions:

1. Show your child the *House* activity page. Ask him who lives in his home.

2. Ask him to draw each family member in the house on his activity page.

Friendship

LOW PREP *Being a Friend Sort*

Materials:

- ☐ Friendship Sort Activity Page (Appendix BB)
- ☐ Crayons
- ☐ Scissors
- ☐ Glue

Directions:

1. Show the *Friendship Sort* activity page to your child. Explain that some of the pictures on the page show people being good friends, while other pictures show people who are not being a good friend.

2. Ask him if he can point to a picture of a good friend.

3. Now, ask him to point to a picture of someone who is not a good friend. Ask him what clues told him that the person was not a good friend.

4. Ask your preschooler to color the pictures and cut them out.

5. Ask your child to sort the pictures into the appropriate columns.

6. Once sorted, he can glue the pictures in place.

LOW PREP *Cotton Ball vs. Sandpaper Words*

Materials:

☐ Cotton Balls   ☐ Sandpaper

Directions:

1. Place a pile of cotton balls in front of your child. Invite him to touch and feel them. He can rub them on his skin.

2. Ask him to describe how the cotton balls feel (soft, fluffy, furry, etc.).

3. Ask your preschooler, "If words were like cotton balls, how would it feel to have the cotton ball words bouncing on your arm?" Ask him what are some soft words that make us feel good (Ex. please, thank you, can I help?, compliments, etc.).

4. Sprinkle the cotton balls over your child's head while you say the soft, cotton ball words.

5. Now, introduce a piece of sandpaper to your child. Ask him to feel it and rub it.

6. Ask him to describe how it feels (rough, hard, spiky, etc.).

7. Ask your preschooler, "If words were like sandpaper, how would it feel to have sandpaper words rubbing against your arm?" Ask him what are some scratchy words that make us feel sad or mad (Ex. mean words, yelling, name calling, etc.).

8. Show your child how sandpaper scratches wood. Tell your child that mean words can "scratch" or injure our feelings. Ask your child how he thinks he would feel if a friend used mean words when talking to him.

9. Give your child a couple of scenarios with friends using nice words and friends using mean words. Ask him to hold up a cotton ball if the friend used a nice word and sandpaper if the friend used a mean word.

◤ LOW PREP ◥ *Fill the Bucket*

Materials:

- ☐ *Have You Filled a Bucket Today?*
  by Carol McCloud
- ☐ Plastic Solo Cup
- ☐ Single Hole Punch
- ☐ Pipe cleaner
- ☐ Stickers
- ☐ Markers

Directions:

1. Read *Have You Filled a Bucket Today?* with your child.

2. Discuss how it's important to be kind to other people because it helps fill up their imaginary happiness bucket, but when we are nice to others it also makes us feel good and fills our own imaginary bucket.

3. Ask him if he would like to make a real bucket.

4. Give him the plastic cup. Allow him to decorate it with stickers and markers.

5. When finished, let your child use the single hole punch to punch a hole at the top of the cup, and a second hole at the top, directly opposite the first hole.

6. Thread the end of the pipe cleaner through the first hole. Wrap it around the hole to tie it in place. Do this again with the other end of the pipe cleaner and the second hole. The pipe cleaner will serve as the handle for your child's bucket.

7. Now your child can fill his bucket with pom poms and each time he chooses to do something nice for someone else he can hand the person a pom pom from his bucket.

LOW PREP *Friendship Bracelet*

Materials:

☐ Yarn
☐ Scissors
☐ 5 Different Colored Pony Beads

Directions:

1. Ask your preschooler if he would enjoy making a friendship bracelet. Explain that even though he is a good friend, it helps to have a reminder of how he should act when he is being a good friend. Sometimes when friends get sad or angry it's hard to remember to be nice. This bracelet will be a good reminder.

2. Use the yarn to measure for a bracelet around your child's wrist. You want it loose enough to tie and slide off of his wrist.

3. Gather five different colored pony beads. Each bead will represent a reminder of being a good friend:

1. Yellow-Slow down before tattling. (Tell an adult if someone is hurt or in danger, but not to tattle on a friend)

2. Red-Be kind with mouth and body.

3. Blue-Be helpful and honest.

4. Green-Share

5. Purple-Let a friend choose what to play.

4. Explain what each color bead means on the bracelet.

5. Allow your preschooler to thread the beads on the yarn. Hold the other end so the beads don't fall off.

6. Tie the bracelet onto your child's wrist.

LOW PREP *Hands are Not for Hitting*

Materials:

- ☐ Hands Are Not For Hitting Activity Page (Appendix BC)
- ☐ Crayons

Directions:

1. Show your preschooler the *Hands Are Not For Hitting* activity page.

2. If possible, sing the jingle at the bottom of the activity page together a few times.

3. Ask your child to place his hands in the box on the activity page. Trace his hands.

4. Allow him to color his hands.

5. Sing the jingle again.

LOW PREP *Pass the Ice Cream*

Materials:

- ☐ *Should I Share My Ice Cream?* by Mo Willems

(Optional)
- ☐ Brown Paper

- ☐ Tape
- ☐ Medium Size Ball

Directions:

1. If you would like, read the book *Should I Share My Ice Cream?* together. This book is a light-hearted way of showing the struggle of deciding to share or not share. In the end, the Elephant decides it's better to share.

2. Roll the brown paper into a cone shape making sure the opening is wide enough for the ball to fit. You will want a cone for your child and yourself.

3. Secure the cone's edges with tape.

4. Place a ball inside the cone.

5. Encourage your child to share his ice cream by passing the ball from his cone to your cone. You and your preschooler can practice saying "please" and "thank you" as you both share the ice cream.

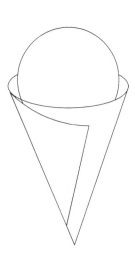

Gardening

LOW PREP *Explore Seeds*

Materials:

☐ Pumpkin   ☐ Pepper
☐ Apple   ☐ Knife
☐ Peach

Directions:

1. You will need four fruits with differing seed sizes. I chose the above fruits because the seeds vary so much, but you will need to choose from what is in season.

2. Cut each fruit in half to expose the seeds.

3. Ask your preschooler to help you extract the seeds from each fruit.

4. Lay the seeds next to each other. Discuss the similarities and differences between each seed.

Flower Counting

Materials:

☐ Flower Activity Pages (Appendix BD)   ☐ Crayons
☐ Scissors   ☐ Glue

Directions:

1. Cut out the numbered petals on the second *Flower* activity page. Shuffle the petals.

2. Show your preschooler the first Flower activity page.

3. Point to the petal with one dot. Ask your child to count the dot.

4. Ask your child to find the petal with the number one on it. Place it over the petal with one dot.

5. Continue Steps 3 and 4 until each petal with dots has a number covering it.

6. Now, your child can glue the petals in place and color the picture.

LOW PREP *Leaf Stamping*

Materials:

☐ Leaves
☐ Paint
☐ Paintbrushes
☐ Paper

Directions:

1. Ask your preschooler to join you on a walk to collect leaves. Collect leaves of different shapes and sizes.

2. After leaves have been collected, take them inside and allow your child to paint the leaves.

3. Ask your child to select a leaf, flip it over onto a piece of paper, and press it down like a stamp.

4. Let your preschooler lift the leaf off the paper to see the print it made.

5. Continue to do this with each leaf to make a beautiful creation.

LOW PREP *Plant Seeds*

Materials:

- ☐ Easy Grow Seeds (Sunflowers, Zinnia, Lettuce, Beans, Marigolds, etc.)
- ☐ Paper Towels
- ☐ Water
- ☐ Large Mason Jar

Directions:

1. Ask your preschooler if he would enjoy planting seeds and watching them grow.

2. Let your child fill the mason jar with paper towels.

3. Gently water the seed jar to wet the paper towels. Do not soak the paper towels.

4. Let your preschooler push seeds down into the paper towels. (If the seeds are positioned around the edge of the jar it is easier for your child to watch the changes that will occur.)

5. Observe the changes each day.

6. If the paper towels start to become dry, carefully add more water to the jar.

7. Once your seeds begin to sprout, form roots, and grow leaves, you can take them out of the mason jar and plant them in soil.

LOW PREP *Seed Names*

Materials:

- ☐ Sunflower Seeds
- ☐ Paper
- ☐ Marker
- ☐ Elmer's Glue

Directions:

1. Write your child's name on a piece of paper.

2. Ask your child if he would enjoy writing his name using sunflower seeds.

3. Allow him to trace his name using the Elmer's glue. (I suggest doing one letter at a time so the glue doesn't dry.)

4. Now ask your child to place the sunflower seeds in the glue outlining his name.

Sort Seeds

Materials:

- ☐ 5-6 Plant Seed Packets
- ☐ Cookie Sheet
- ☐ Ice Cube Tray
- ☐ Scissors

Directions:

1. Before you begin the activity with your preschooler, place one seed from each seed packet in a different cup of the ice cube tray. Cut out a small picture of what the seed grows into from the seed packet and place it inside the cup with the seed.

2. Now, pour all of the seed packets onto a cookie sheet. Mix them together.

3. Invite your preschooler to look at the seeds. Explain that you have a big problem and need his help sorting the seeds into the correct groups.

4. Show him which seeds go in each ice cube cup to match the correct plant.

This is an excellent activity to practice identification and categorizing for math skills. It also develops fine motor skills and concentration.

Healthy Habits

LOW PREP *Blow Paint Germ Hands*

Materials:

☐ Paper
☐ Marker

☐ Watercolor
   Paint

☐ Paintbrush
☐ Straw

Directions:

This activity is best to do outside.

1. Trace your child's hands on to a piece of paper.

2. Now ask your preschooler to use a paintbrush to drop a few drips of watercolor paint onto his hands, but don't paint the hands.

   **If you do not have watercolor paint, you can use watered down washable paint.

3. Now, ask your preschooler to use the straw to blow the paint around the hands. Explain that this is similar to what happens when someone sneezes. The germs spread out, so it's important to wash our hands.

Brush Away Letters

Materials:

☐ Tooth Activity Page (Appendix BE)
☐ Sheet Protector or Laminator

☐ Dry Erase Marker
☐ Toothbrush

Directions:

1. You will need to laminate the *Tooth* activity page. If you do not have a laminator, then you can place the activity page inside a sheet protector.

2. Write letters on the laminated tooth in random order. (You can also write numbers or shapes.)

3. Invite your preschooler to help you brush all of the sugar bugs (letters) off the tooth by using the toothbrush to erase the letters you call out.

4. Begin with "A." Once he locates "A" ask him to use his toothbrush to erase the letter.

5. Continue until all letters are erased.

Egg Brushing Experiment

Materials:

- ☐ Clear Cups
- ☐ Dark Soda
- ☐ Toothbrush
- ☐ Toothpaste
- ☐ Hard Boiled Egg

Directions:

1. Place the hardboiled egg in a cup of dark soda (you can also use coffee). Make sure the soda covers the entire egg. Place the cup in a safe location for 12 hours.

2. Show your child the egg in the soda. Ask him to pretend that the egg is his teeth. Explain that when he drinks a lot of soda that the soda sticks to his teeth.

3. Pull the egg out of the soda cup.

4. Ask your preschooler to use the toothbrush without toothpaste to try to brush the soda off the egg.

5. Now allow him to brush the egg (tooth) with toothpaste, toothbrush and water. Let him observe the results.

6. Ask your preschooler if the tooth became cleaner using toothpaste. Did the tooth become all the way clean? Does he think soda is good for his teeth?

LOW PREP *Fruit and Vegetable Patterns*

Materials:

☐ Fruit and Vegetable Pattern Activity Page (Appendix BF)
☐ Scissors
☐ Glue

Directions:

1. Show your preschooler the *Fruit and Vegetable Pattern* activity page. Explain that fruits and vegetables help make people grow big and strong.

2. Ask your child if he can recognize the vegetables on the page. Ask him which vegetables he enjoys eating.

3. Ask him if he can identify the fruits on the page. Ask him which fruits he enjoys eating.

4. Ask your preschooler to cut out the extra fruit and vegetable pieces at the bottom of the page.

5. Point to the first pattern. State each vegetable in the pattern. When you reach the end of the pattern ask your preschooler which vegetable would come next in the pattern.

6. Ask him to place the vegetable in the question mark box.

7. Complete Steps 5 and 6 for each pattern.

8. Once the patterns are complete, he can glue the fruits and vegetables in place.

LOW PREP *Germ Washing Station*

Materials:

☐ Plastic Bin
☐ Soap
☐ Sponges
☐ Small Porcupine Balls (Optional)

Directions:

1. Fill the plastic bin with water, soap, and the small porcupine balls. The porcupine balls represent germs; however, if you do not have any, your preschooler can just wash his favorite toys.

2. Invite your preschooler to play in the washing station. Allow him to wash his favorite toys.

3. Explain to your child that he is washing away germs that can get stuck on toys.

LOW PREP *Healthy Food Beginning Sounds*

Materials:

☐ Healthy Food Beginning Sounds Activity Page (Appendix BG)
☐ Pencil

Directions:

1. Show your preschooler the *Healthy Food Beginning Sounds* activity page. Talk to your child about healthy foods—what is healthy food, examples of healthy food, why it's important to eat healthy food. Ask him to identify healthy foods he enjoys eating.

2. Point to the first picture on the activity page. Ask your preschooler to say the name of the food.

3. Ask him if he can identify the sound and letter at the beginning of the word.

4. Ask him to trace over the letter.

5. Continue to do this for the food in the first column of the activity page.

6. For the food in the second column, follow Steps 2 and 3, but this time he will write the letter on his own. If he needs assistance, add dotted letters for him to trace over.

LOW PREP *Healthy vs. Unhealthy Sort*

Materials:
☐ Healthy vs. Unhealthy Activity Page (Appendix BH)
☐ Crayons

Directions:
1. Show your preschooler the *Healthy vs. Unhealthy* activity page. (Review the same information about healthy and unhealthy food options you discussed with your child in the Healthy Food Beginning Sounds).

2. Instruct your preschooler to color the healthy foods on the activity page and cross out the unhealthy foods.

3. Explain that unhealthy foods often taste good, but the unhealthy foods do not help make his body big and strong. That is why it is better to only occasionally eat unhealthy food; the less the better.

LOW PREP *Inside and Outside Fruit Match*

Materials:
☐ Inside and Outside Fruit Activity Page (Appendix BI)
☐ Scissors
☐ Glue

Directions:
1. Explain to your preschooler that he will help you match the outside of fruit to what it looks like on the inside.

2. Show him the *Inside and Outside Fruit* activity page.

3. Point to each fruit on the first activity page. Ask him to identify the fruit.

4. Now, ask him to cut out the inside fruit pictures on the second activity page.

5. Point to the first image on the first activity page. Ask him if he can find the inside picture for that fruit.

6. Place it in the "inside" column and glue it down.

7. Complete Steps 5 and 6 until each fruit is matched.

LOW PREP *Toothbrush Writing*

Materials:

- ☐ Tray with Edges
- ☐ Salt
- ☐ Toothbrush
- ☐ Flash Cards (Optional)

Directions:

1. Pour salt onto the tray.

2. Invite your preschooler to practice writing in the salt using a toothbrush.

3. Ask your child to copy the letter or numbers on the flash cards. He can draw shapes that you call out as well. He can also draw pictures in the salt.

LOW PREP *Workout Rotation*

Directions:

1. Invite your preschooler to do a workout with you. Explain that when he moves his body it helps to build his muscles and make the muscles stronger so he can carry his favorite toy, run on the playground, or ride a bike.

2. Here are some exercises that you can do with your preschooler:

   1. Do 5 squats.

   2. Stand on one foot for 10 seconds. Now stand on the other foot for 10 seconds.

   3. Do 3 push-ups.

   4. Do 10 mountain climbers.

   5. Crab walk across the room.

   6. Do arm circles for 1 minute.

   7. Do lunges across the room.

   8. Lie on your back and pedal your feet for 20 seconds.

   9. Frog hop across the room.

   10. Plank for 20 seconds.

   Add in your own exercise ideas, as well.

Money

LOW PREP *Clean Coins*

Materials:

☐ Plastic Bin
☐ Soap
☐ Water
☐ Sponges
☐ Old Toothbrush
☐ Coins

Directions:

1. Fill a plastic bin with water and soap.

2. Invite your child to clean the coins in the water bucket. He may use sponges, toothbrushes, rags, etc.

3. This is a great way to introduce money to your child. As he is cleaning and touching each type of coin, tell him the name of the coin and its value.

4. As he continues to clean, begin to ask him which coin he is cleaning.

LOW PREP *Coin Boats*

Materials:
- ☐ Aluminum Foil
- ☐ Coins
- ☐ Bucket of Water

Directions:

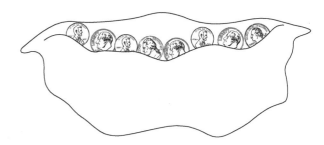

1. Ask your preschooler if he would like to make a boat.

2. Explain to him that you will give him a piece of aluminum foil and he will need to form the foil into a boat that can float in water while holding coins. You can create a boat to show him an example.

3. Tear off a piece of aluminum foil approximately a foot long.

4. Let your preschooler fold up the edges to form his boat.

5. Let him place his boat in the water to test if it floats. Let him make adjustments if needed.

6. Once his boat floats, allow him to add coins to his boat. Count how many coins he can place in his boat before it begins to sink.

7. For additional fun, your preschooler can make four boats and compare how many of each type of coin a boat will hold before sinking. Let him place only pennies in one boat, nickels in a separate boat, dimes in a separate boat, and quarters in a separate boat. Allow him to see which boat holds the most coins before sinking.

LOW PREP *Coin Counting*

Materials:

- ☐ Coin Counting Activity Page (Appendix BJ)
- ☐ Coins

Directions:

1. Show your preschooler the *Coin Counting* activity page.

2. Ask him to help you read the sentence in the first box.

3. Now instruct him to place the correct amount of the correct coin in the box. If your preschooler needs a challenge, add up the value of the coins in the box (assist as needed).

4. Complete Steps 2 and 3 for each box on the activity page.

Coin Deposit Bank

Materials:

- ☐ Cereal Box
- ☐ Wrapping Paper
- ☐ Tape
- ☐ Marker
- ☐ Scissors
- ☐ Coins

Directions:

1. Wrap an empty cereal box in wrapping paper.

2. On the wide side of the cereal box cut four slits in the box. The slits should be big enough to insert a quarter.

3. Above the first slit tape a penny. Above the second slit tape a nickel. Above the third slit tape a dime. Above the fourth slit tape a quarter.

4. Above each coin on the cereal box write the value of the coin.

5. Invite your preschooler to be a banker that deposits money into the bank you created.

6. He will need to deposit the coins into the matching slot.

7. As he is depositing coins, ask him the names and values of each coin.

Coin Eggs

Materials:

☐ Plastic Eggs   ☐ Coins

Directions:

1. Fill ten plastic eggs with coins. Each egg should only contain one type of coin. The coins should not be mixed. For example, you can fill one egg with ten pennies and another egg with 7 dimes.

2. After the eggs are filled, ask your preschooler to choose an egg to open.

3. When he opens the egg ask him to identify the coin and then count how many coins are in the egg.

4. Do this until all eggs have been counted.

Coin Letters

Materials:

☐ 4 Pieces of Paper
☐ Marker
☐ Coins

Directions:

1. Write the following letters on a piece of paper in large uppercase letters—"P, N, D, and Q." Each piece of paper should only have one letter written on it.

2. Ask your preschooler to trace the letters with coins.

3. He will use pennies to trace the "P." Use pennies to outline the "P."

4. He will use nickels to trace the "N." Use nickels to outline the "N."

5. He will use dimes to trace the "D." Use dimes to outline the "D."

6. He will use quarters to trace the "Q." Use quarters to outline the "Q."

7. As he is tracing you can ask him to tell you the name of the letter and coin. You can tell him that the coin begins with that letter.

LOW PREP Coin Matching

Materials:

- ☐ Piggy Bank Activity Page (Appendix BK)
- ☐ Coins

Directions:

1. Show your preschooler the *Piggy Bank* activity page. Explain that each type of coin is located in the piggy bank and he will need to place real coins on the pictures on the activity page.

2. Ask him to pick up a coin. Ask him to identify the coin he picked up.

3. Now, ask him to place the coin on a matching coin on the activity page.

4. Complete Steps 3 and 4 until the piggy bank is full.

LOW PREP Coin Sorting

Materials:

- ☐ Coin Sorting Activity Page (Appendix BL)
- ☐ Coins

Directions:

1. Show your preschooler the *Coin Sorting* activity page. Explain that he will be in charge of separating the coins into their own boxes.

2. Point to each box and tell him which coins goes in each box. You can even place the first coin in each box to help him get started.

3. Allow him to sort as many coins as he would enjoy.

LOW PREP *Coin Stack*

Materials:

☐ Coins
☐ Dice

Directions:

1. Ask your preschooler if he would enjoy building a tall tower using coins.

2. Ask him to roll a die and count the dots on the die.

3. Ask him to count the same number (Step 2) of coins.

4. Tell him he can use the coins to begin creating a tower.

5. Repeat Steps 2-5 to continue adding to his tower.

6. Let him see how tall he can make the tower before it falls down.

LOW PREP *Don't Break the Bank*

Materials:

☐ Don't Break the Bank Activity Page (Appendix BM)
☐ Coins
☐ Dice

Directions:

1. Ask your preschooler if he would enjoy playing a game.

2. Show him the *Don't Break the Bank* activity page.

3. Explain to your child that he will roll the die, and count the dots on the die. Next, he will place a coin that matches the roll onto the piggy bank.

4. If he rolls a two, he must clear the piggy bank and start over because it "broke the bank."

5. Free choice means that he can pick any coin he wants and place it in the piggy bank.

6. He can play as many times as he would enjoy.

Opposites

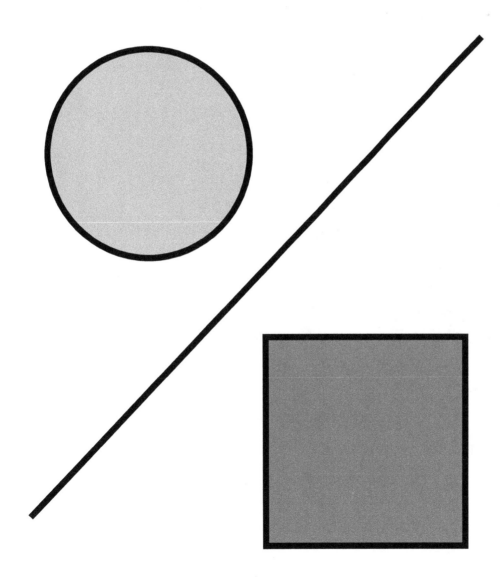

Foot Trail

Materials:

- ☐ *The Foot Book* by Dr. Seuss (Optional)
- ☐ Construction Paper
- ☐ Markers
- ☐ Scissors

Directions:

1. You will need to make 14 of the "foot" cut-outs. You should be able to get three or four cut-outs from one piece of construction paper.

2. Label each foot with the following words: wet, dry, left, right, day, night, high, low, front, back, slow, fast, small, and big. Draw picture clues under each word to help your child "read" the word.

3. Split each opposite pair so that you have two piles of words. (In the first pile you should have the words: wet, left, day, high, front, slow, and small. In the second pile you should have the words: dry, right, night, low, back, fast, and big.)

4. Place one pile in a central location.

5. Take the other pile and make a trail for your child to follow.

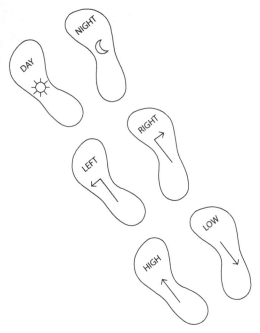

6. Read *The Foot Book* by Dr. Seuss with your preschooler. Explain that the book talks about opposites. Tell him that hot is the opposite of cold.

7. Now invite your child to play a game with you where he will begin at the first foot on the trail.

8. Ask him to read the word or look at the picture to read the word.

9. Ask him for the opposite of the word he read from Step 8.

10. Now he will go to the central pile to find the correct opposite match. Bring the foot back and place it beside its opposite.

11. Continue until all opposites are matched.

LOW PREP *Opposites Board Game*

Materials:

- ☐ Opposites Board Game Activity Page (Appendix BN)
- ☐ Dice
- ☐ Game Pieces

Directions:

1. Ask your preschooler if he would enjoy playing a game with you.

2. Show him the *Opposites Board Game* activity page.

3. Place your game pieces on "Start."

4. Take turns rolling the die. If the player who rolled the die lands on a picture, he should say it's name and it's opposite. (Assist your child as needed.)

5. If a player lands on a number, go backwards or forwards the correct number of spaces.

6. The first player to "Finish" wins.

LOW PREP *Opposites Coloring*

Materials:

- ☐ Opposites Coloring Activity Page (Appendix BO)
- ☐ Crayons

Directions:

1. Show your preschooler the *Opposites Coloring* activity page.

2. Point out that each picture on the left-hand side of the activity page has an opposite that he will need to find on the right-hand side of the activity page.

3. When your child finds the match he will need to color the circle beside the picture the same color as the circle on the left side.

    For example, if the day time picture on the left-hand side has a yellow circle beside it, your child will locate the night time picture on the right side of the activity page and color the circle yellow.

4. Complete each opposites match.

LOW PREP *Opposites Day*

Directions:

1. When your child wakes up, announce that the day will be Opposite Day. This means that everything will be done the opposite of a normal day. Here are some examples:

   1. Wear summer clothes during winter or winter clothes during summer.

   2. Wear clothes backwards instead of forwards.

   3. Take a bath in the morning instead of at night or at night instead of in the morning.

   4. Eat dinner for breakfast and breakfast for dinner.

   5. Eat dessert before dinner.

   6. Allow your child to be the parent while you are the child.

LOW PREP *Simon Says Opposites*

Directions:

1. Invite your preschooler to play "Simon Says," but with a twist. When you call out an instruction, he will do the opposite.

2. Call out an instruction. (Ex. Simon Says turn on the light.)

3. Your preschooler will need to think of the opposite of your instructions, and do it. (He will turn the light off.)

4. If your child does the exact instruction you gave him, he is out and he can be Simon.

Simple
Machines

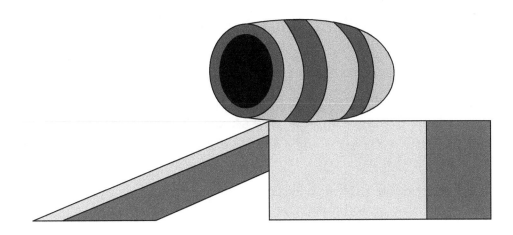

Inclined Plane Art

Materials:

- ☐ Paper Towel Tube
- ☐ Scissors
- ☐ Block
- ☐ Toy Cars
- ☐ Paint
- ☐ Paper Plate
- ☐ Poster Board or Roll of Paper

Directions:

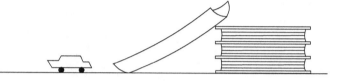

1. Place the paper over the top of the table. You will want the entire table covered.

   **This activity might get messy, so you may want to do it outside.

2. Cut the paper towel tube in half so that it creates two U-shaped ramps.

3. Place a block at one end of the table. Place each half of the paper towel tube on the block to form a ramp.

4. Squirt washable paint on to a paper plate.

5. Ask your preschooler if he would like to learn about a simple machine that helps make work easier. Explain that you have set up an inclined plane (ramp). Inclined planes help objects move from a higher location to a lower location more easily than carrying it.

6. Show your preschooler that he will dip his car in the paint, and then roll it down the inclined plane (paper towel tube) to create art.

7. He may do this as many times as he wishes.

Launching Balls

Materials:

- ☐ Ping Pong Balls
- ☐ Wooden Yardstick (or Something Similar)
- ☐ Large Can (Soup Can, Coffee Can)
- ☐ Plastic Cup
- ☐ Duct Tape

Directions:

1. Tape the plastic cup on one end of the yardstick. Make sure the cup is taped down securely and the tape is positioned where objects can still be placed in the cup.

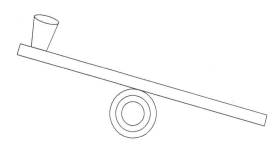

2. Ask your preschooler if he would enjoy learning about a machine that helps him launch balls. Invite him to go outside with you for this activity.

3. Place the large can on the ground sideways so that it can roll. Explain to your preschooler that the can is called the fulcrum. The fulcrum is where the lever (yardstick) pivots. It helps make it easier to lift heavy objects.

4. Place the yardstick over the can with the plastic cup facing up. The yardstick is the lever of the machine that moves the object. This lever is moving the ping pong ball.

5. Ask your child to place a ping pong ball in the plastic cup.

6. Make sure the cup end of the yardstick is resting on the ground, and then have your preschooler push down on the opposite end of the yardstick with his hand or foot.

7. Your child can adjust where the yardstick sits on the can to test which position makes the ping pong ball launch farther. (Be creative by setting a basket in the yard, or several containers which have various values, as targets. It can be great fun!)

LOW PREP *Playground Pulley*

Materials:

- ☐ Bucket with Handle
- ☐ String
- ☐ Scissors

Directions:

1. Help your preschooler create a pulley. You may use a railing of playground equipment.

2. First, cut a string about 8 feet long depending on the height of railing you plan to use.

3. Then, help your preschooler tie one end of a string around the handle of a bucket.

4. Thread the other end of the string through the railing. Loop it around the rail one time. Tie the end of the string to the base of the playground equipment so the string doesn't become loose.

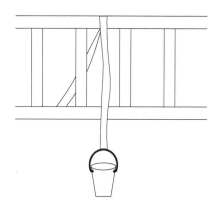

5. Allow your preschooler to place an object inside the bucket.

6. He will then need to walk up the playground to the looped string. Ask him to begin pulling the string towards him. He should see the bucket begin to rise up off the ground and travel towards him.

7. Explain that he has created a pulley. Pulleys help people lift or lower things that might be too heavy. Think about an elevator—elevators carry people to different floors.

8. Allow your child to test out his pulley with different size objects in his bucket.

LOW PREP *Wedge Experiment*

Materials:

- ☐ Paper
- ☐ Tape
- ☐ Sharpened Pencil
- ☐ 2 Shoe Boxes

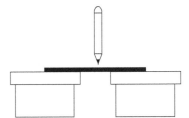

Directions:

1. Explain to your preschooler that a wedge is an inclined plane that is thick at one end and goes to a point on the other (e.g., a door stop, an ax, the point of a pencil). Today he will get to test if a wedge makes breaking a piece of paper easier or not.

2. Place two shoe boxes beside each other about 6 inches apart.

3. Place the piece of paper across the two boxes like a bridge. Tape the piece of paper to the boxes.

4. Ask your preschooler to hold the pencil over the paper, eraser side touching the paper. Ask him to try to push the eraser through the paper. You may have to hold the boxes steady as your preschooler pushes the pencil down. Ask your child if it is easy to break the paper with a flat surface?

5. Now ask him to turn the pencil over so the wedge (sharpened side of the pencil) is touching the paper. Ask him to push the point of the pencil down through the paper to try to break the paper. Was he successful?

Wheel and Axel Car

Materials:

- ☐ Toilet Paper Tube
- ☐ Cereal Box
- ☐ Single Hole Punch
- ☐ 2 Straws
- ☐ Scissors
- ☐ 2 Pipe Cleaners
- ☐ Paint
- ☐ Paintbrushes

Directions:

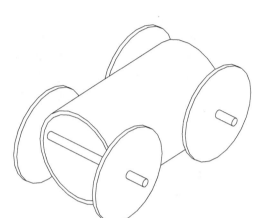

1. Ask your preschooler if he would like to make a race car to learn about wheel and axel machines.

2. First, draw four wheels on the cereal box. You can make the wheels about 3 inches in diameter. Cut the wheels out.

3. Allow your preschooler to paint the toilet paper tube and wheels. Let the items dry.

4. Once dry, use the hole punch to make four holes in the toilet paper tube. Your preschooler can assist with this task. You will need two at the front of the tube on direct opposite sides, and two at the back of the tube on direct opposite sides.

5. Cut two pieces of straw, each measuring 3 ½ inches long.

6. Cut two pieces of pipe cleaner each measuring 4 inches long.

7. Ask your preschooler to slide the straws through the front holes and the back holes of the toilet paper tube. These are the axels. The axels hold the wheels in place and spin with the wheels.

8. Slide each pipe cleaner through each axel (straw).

9. Now, use the hole punch to punch a hole in the center of each wheel.

10. Slide each wheel onto each end of the straws.

11. Fold the extra pipe cleaner over the end of the straw to prevent the wheels from coming loose.

12. Allow your preschooler to zoom his car around.

Scissor Skills

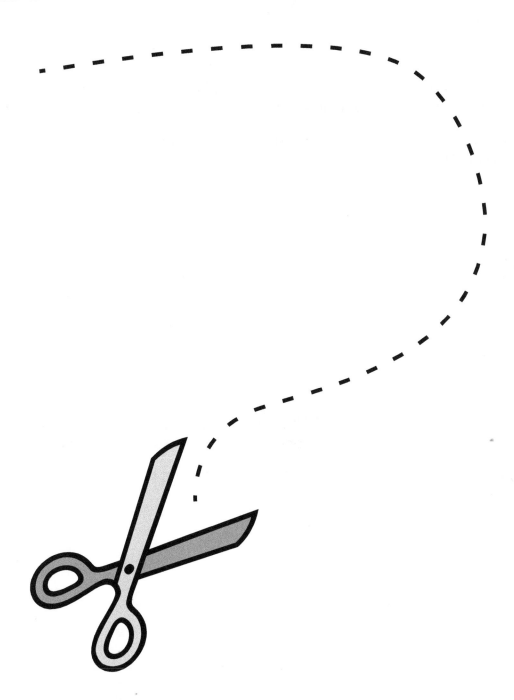

A helpful tip for teaching your preschooler to use scissors is to draw a smiley face on his thumbnail. Tell him that he should always be able to see the smiley face when he is cutting. This will remind him to keep his hand in the right position.

LOW PREP *Cut Gummy Worms*

Materials:

- ☐ Scissors
- ☐ Gummy Worms

Directions:

1. Present your preschooler with a small amount of gummy worms and a pair of child's scissors. Ask him if he would like to use the scissors to cut the gummy worms.

2. Before cutting, remind him of the importance of scissor safety and how to hold the scissors properly.

LOW PREP *Cut Junk Mail*

Materials:

- ☐ Scissors
- ☐ Junk Mail

Directions:

1. Ask your preschooler if he could be your helper and cut the junk mail into tiny pieces. Remind him that he may only cut the mail that you give him.

2. Instruct him on how to hold his scissors, and then let him cut the mail.

The Ultimate Preschool Activity Guide | Autumn McKay

LOW PREP *Cut Paint Samples*

Materials:

☐ Scissors
☐ Paint Samples

Directions:

1. Next time you are at the hardware store collect an assortment of paint samples.

2. Invite your preschooler to cut the different shades of colors apart. If he is adept in "scissor skills" ask him to cut along the white border of the paint samples.

3. Remind him of the correct way to hold scissors before he begins cutting.

LOW PREP *Cut Playdough*

Materials:

☐ Scissors
☐ Playdough

Directions:

1. Roll playdough into "snakes."

2. Ask your preschooler if he would enjoy cutting apart the playdough snakes.

3. Remind him of the correct hand position for holding scissors.

Cut and Rescue

Materials:

- ☐ Scissors
- ☐ Muffin Pan
- ☐ Painter's Tape
- ☐ Small Toys

Directions:

1. Place the small toys inside the muffin pan cups.

2. Run painter's tape across each muffin cup vertically and horizontally.

3. Tell your preschooler that the toys are captured and they need to be rescued. Ask your preschooler if he can rescue the toys by cutting them out of the traps.

4. Allow your preschooler to cut the tape and rescue each toy.

Cut Spaghetti

Materials:

- ☐ Scissors
- ☐ Cooked Spaghetti

Directions:

1. Cook a box of spaghetti.

2. Let it cool.

3. Invite your preschooler to use scissors to cut the spaghetti.

4. Remind him how to hold scissors correctly.

LOW PREP *Cut Straws*

Materials:
☐ Scissors
☐ Straws

Directions:
1. Place a bunch of straws on the table. Allow your preschooler to use his scissors to cut them any length he desires. It's fun to cut straws because the straws shoot off as they are cut.

2. Remind him to hold his scissors so that his thumb faces upwards.

Sports

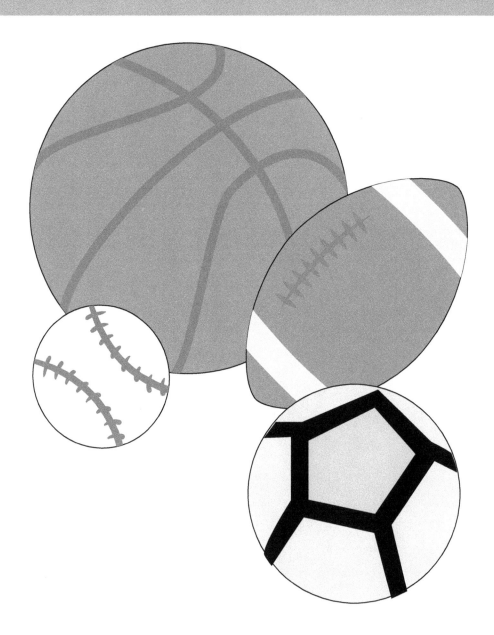

LOW PREP *Baseball Prewriting*

Materials:

☐ Baseball Activity Page (Appendix BP)
☐ Crayons

Directions:

1. Show your preschooler the *Baseball* activity page. Explain that the baseballs need help finding their way to the baseball gloves.

2. Ask your preschooler to use a crayon to trace each line from the baseball to the baseball glove.

Basketball Counting

Materials:

☐ Basketball Counting Activity Page (Appendix BQ)
☐ Scissors
☐ Orange Pom Poms or Counters

Directions:

1. Cut out each basketball goal from the *Basketball Counting* activity page.

2. Set out the basketball goals in order from 1-10.

3. Ask your preschooler if he would enjoy scoring basketball goals. Explain that he will need to read the number on the basketball goal. then place the same number of basketballs (orange pom poms) on the card.

4. Encourage him as he fills in the basketballs on each card.

Football Letter Hunt

Materials:

- ☐ Football Activity Page (Appendix BR)
- ☐ Scissors
- ☐ Laminator or Sheet Protector
- ☐ Dry Erase Marker

Directions:

1. First, cut out the football from the *Football* activity page.

2. Now, laminate the Football activity. If you do not have a laminator, insert the activity page into a sheet protector.

3. Use your dry erase marker to write letters all over the picture in random order. You can choose to write numbers too.

4. Ask your preschooler if he would enjoy playing a football game. Explain that you will call out a letter and he will need to locate the letter and cover it with the football. If the ball lands on a letter between the goal post then he will score a field goal (3 points).

5. Call out the letters in alphabetical order.

6. When your child locates the letter, ask him if he scored a field goal or not.

7. Calculate his score at the end of the activity.

Mini Ice Hockey

Materials:

☐ 9x13" Pan
☐ Water
☐ Bottle Cap
☐ 2 Plastic Spoons
☐ Legos

Directions:

1. Fill your 9"x13" pan with about 3 inches of water. Place the pan on a flat surface in the freezer. Allow the water to completely freeze.

2. Build two goals (similar to a bridge shape) out of Legos.

3. Once the water is frozen, take the pan out of the freezer and set up the hockey rink. Place the goals on either end of the pan.

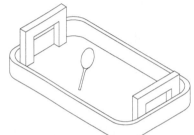

4. Invite your preschooler to play you in a game of hockey. Place the bottle cap in the middle of the ice. Hand your child a plastic spoon.

5. Instruct him to use his spoon to hit the puck (bottle cap) into his goal (the one you are guarding). You will try to defend the goal.

6. Take turns trying to make goals while the other playing defends the goal.

7. The first person to five points wins.

Paper Plate Skating

LOW PREP

Materials:

☐ Paper Plates

Directions:

1. Ask your preschooler if he would enjoy being an ice skater or hockey player today. Explain that you will provide him with some ice skates that he will get to use to slide around the floor.

2. Place the paper plates on the uncarpeted floor. Ask him to place his bare feet on the skates and begin to slide around.

3. He can twirl, race, try to play hockey, or anything else he enjoys. This is a great exercise to build the big muscles (gross motor skills) in his little body.

LOW PREP *Soccer Ball Math*

Materials:

- ☐ Plastic Cups
- ☐ Marker
- ☐ Soccer Ball

Directions:

1. Hold the plastic cups opening face down. Write numbers 1-5 on the plastic cups.

2. Set the plastic cups up on one end of the yard. Set the cups about a foot apart from each other.

3. Ask your preschooler to stand 10 feet away from the cups.

4. Place a soccer ball at his feet.

5. Ask him to kick the soccer ball to knock down one cup.

6. Ask him to kick the soccer ball to knock down a second cup.

7. Hold up the two cups for him to read the numbers. Now ask him to add (or subtract) the two numbers. For example, if he knocks down the "2" and "3" cup, you will ask him what is 2+3?

8. You can hold up the same amount of fingers on each of your hands if he needs to count to find the sum. (Two fingers on one hand and three fingers on the other hand)

9. Set the cups up and repeat Steps 5-8 as many times as he enjoys.

Spy
Training

LOW PREP *Fingerprint Science*

Materials:

☐ Ink Pad
☐ Balloons

Directions:

1. Explain to your preschooler that when spies go on a mission they often gather the fingerprints that are left in a room. Using the fingerprints, the spy can determine the number of people in the room and the identity of the various people. Tell your child that today he will investigate fingerprints like a spy.

2. Ask your child to press his index finger in the ink pad and stamp it onto the flat balloon.

3. Make sure the ink is dry. Then, blow the balloon up and tie it.

4. Ask your preschooler to look at the lines running through the fingerprint.

5. Now, place your index finger in the ink pad and stamp it onto another flat balloon.

6. Blow up the balloon and tie it.

7. Hold the fingerprints next to each other. Point out the difference in your preschooler's fingerprint and your fingerprint.

The Ultimate Preschool Activity Guide | Autumn McKay

LOW PREP *Invisible Ink Message*

Materials:

☐ Milk   ☐ Paintbrush   ☐ Heat Source
☐ Bowl   ☐ Paper

Directions:

1. Explain to your preschooler that spies have to make secret messages to share with other spies. Spies make their messages "secret" so non-spies cannot read them.

2. Place a plain white piece of paper in front of your child.

3. Pour milk into a small bowl. (The more fat in the milk, the better.)

4. Ask your child to use his paintbrush to write a secret message using the milk as his ink.

5. Allow the milk to dry.

6. You will need a heat source (lamps, iron, etc.) to read the secret message. An adult needs to be responsible for the heat source. Hold the heat source over the secret message to reveal it.

Laser Beam Obstacle

Materials:

☐ Red Streamer or Yarn
☐ Painter's Tape

Directions:

1. Create an obstacle course across one of the rooms in your house using streamers and tape. You want the streamers to criss-cross and be high and low.

2. After you have created the obstacle course, explain to your preschooler that these are pretend lasers that he must cross without touching.

3. Have him start on one side of the room and make it the other side of the room. If he touches a laser beam he needs to start over.

LOW PREP *Secret Code Message*

Materials:

- ☐ Secret Code Activity Page (Appendix BS)
- ☐ Pencil

Directions:

1. Show your preschooler the *Secret Code* activity page.

2. Tell him that he will look at the picture at the top of the page to decide what letter to write into each blank.

3. After he solves all of the clues, it will reveal a secret message for the little spy.

4. Help guide him through the clues as needed.

LOW PREP *What's Missing?*

Materials:

- ☐ Cookie Sheet
- ☐ Small Toys

Directions:

1. Place a variety of small toys on a cookie sheet.

2. Explain to your preschooler that spies need to be very observant, which means they need to pay attention to their surroundings.

3. Show your preschooler the cookie sheet with the small toys. Give him two minutes to observe the toys on the tray.

4. Ask him to turn around or close his eyes so he cannot see the tray.

5. Remove and hide one of the toys from the cookie tray.

6. Ask your preschooler to open his eyes or turn back around to inspect the cookie sheet.

7. Ask him what toy is missing.

8. Repeat Steps 3-7 until all toys have been removed.

Water

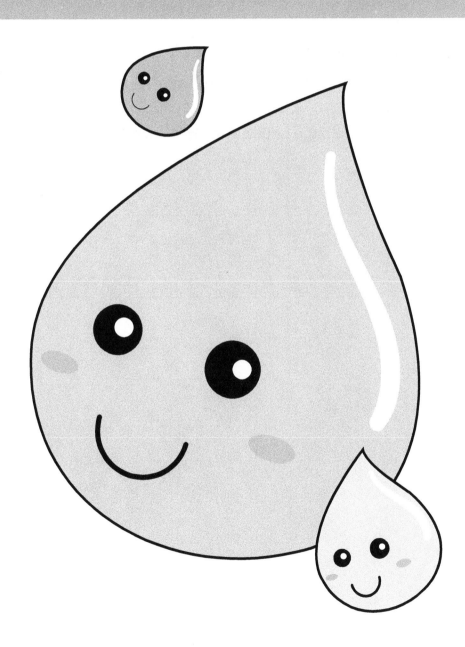

LOW PREP *Frozen Paintbrushes*

Materials:

☐ Ice Cube Tray ☐ Popsicle Sticks ☐ Washable Paint

Directions:

1. To prepare the paintbrushes, fill the ice cube tray with a few drops of paint in each cup. Add water. Stir the mixture.

2. Break the popsicle sticks in half. Place one half popsicle stick into each ice cube tray cup.

3. Place paint mixtures in freezer until completely frozen.

4. Once frozen, remove the frozen paintbrushes from the ice cube tray.

5. Invite your preschooler to use the frozen paintbrushes to paint the sidewalk or a piece of paper. He may hold the popsicle sticks as handles.

LOW PREP *Keep Paper Dry Experiment*

Materials:

- ☐ Medium Bucket of Water
- ☐ Glass Cup
- ☐ Paper Towel

Directions:

1. Ask your preschooler what would happen if he placed a paper towel in a bucket of water.

2. Have him place the paper towel in the water to see if his prediction was accurate.

3. Now, ask your child to place a scrunched up paper towel in the bottom of the glass cup. Make sure it is scrunched tight to the bottom of the glass.

4. Ask him what he thinks will happen to the paper towel when the glass goes in the water.

5. Flip the glass upside down, holding it straight down; put the glass in the bucket of water. Make sure the glass is touching the bottom of the bucket.

6. Pull the glass straight out of the water.

7. Ask your preschooler to touch the paper towel to observe what happened (It stayed dry.).

LOW PREP *Leak Proof Bag*

Materials:

☐ Plastic Ziploc Bag ☐ Sharp Pencils ☐ Water

Directions:

1. Fill the Ziploc bag ¾ full with water and seal it closed.

2. Tell your preschooler that you bet that he can poke a pencil through the bag and the water won't leak out.

3. Take the bag of water outside along with the sharp pencils.

4. Ask your preschooler to gently stab the pencil through the bag so that it pierces both sides. (Be extra careful so that no one is harmed during this experiment.)

5. Allow your child time to investigate if the water will leak out where the pencil is located in the bag.

6. Then he can stab more pencils through the bag.

Monster Battle

Materials:

☐ Chalk ☐ Squirt Bottle ☐ Water

Directions:

1. Using chalk, draw monsters on the driveway. (If you don't feel confident in your monster drawing abilities, then consider drawing numbers or letters.)

2. Tell your preschooler you need his help fighting off the monsters that are in the driveway.

3. Hand your child a squirt bottle filled with water and let him squirt each monster until it washes away.

4. This is a fun way to build his fine motor skills needed for writing.

LOW PREP *Oil and Water*

Materials:

- ☐ 3-4 Cups of Water
- ☐ Eye Dropper
- ☐ Food Coloring
- ☐ Pan
- ☐ Baby Oil

Directions:

1. Ask your preschooler if he would like to see what happens if you mix oil and water together.

2. Begin by filling three or four cups with water. Allow your child to pick a food coloring to add to each cup. Stir the water.

3. Fill the bottom of a pan with baby oil.

4. Now allow your preschooler to use an eye dropper to suck up the colored water and squirt it into the baby oil.

5. Let him create an oil and water design.

LOW PREP *Walking Water*

Materials:

☐ 7 Clear Cups
☐ Paper Towels
☐ Food Coloring
☐ Water
☐ Scissors

Directions:

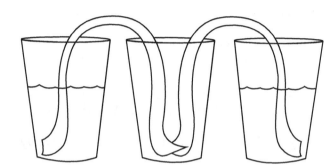

1. Ask your preschooler if he would like to see water walk. Let him help you get the supplies and materials ready.

2. Place the seven cups in a straight row.

3. Pour water into the first, third, fifth, and seventh cup. Fill the cups 7/8 full with water.

4. Add five drops of red food coloring to the first and seventh cup.

5. Add five drops of yellow food coloring to the third cup.

6. Add five drops of blue food coloring to the fifth cup.

7. If you are using pick-a-piece paper towels, you will need to fold the paper towel in half lengthwise once and then twice. If you are using full sheet paper towels, then you will need to cut the full sheet in half first. Then fold it in half lengthwise once and then twice. You will need six folded paper towels.

8. Trim the ends of the paper towels so there is not excess paper towel sticking in the air when resting between cups.

9. Place one half of the rolled paper towel in the first cup and the other half in the second cup. Then another folded paper towel in the second cup and third cup, and so on. There should be a folded paper towel lying over each cup rim, connecting the cups.

10. Watch what begins to happen. The colored water should begin to crawl up the paper towel into the next cup. When the water from both cups meets it will begin to mix into a new color.

LOW PREP *Water Absorption*

Materials:

- ☐ Sponge
- ☐ Styrofoam
- ☐ Napkin
- ☐ Wax Paper
- ☐ Sock
- ☐ Ziploc Bag
- ☐ Construction paper
- ☐ Aluminum Foil
- ☐ Cotton Balls
- ☐ Eye Dropper
- ☐ Bowl of Colored Water

Directions:

1. Set out all of the materials. Explain to your preschooler that he will determine which items absorb or soak up water.

2. Allow him to fill the eye dropper with the colored water so he can squeeze the water on each material one at a time.

3. Each time he uses the eye dropper, ask him if the material absorbed the water.

LOW PREP *What Dissolves in Water?*

Materials:

- ☐ Small Bowls
- ☐ Flour
- ☐ Sugar
- ☐ Rice
- ☐ Cornmeal
- ☐ Oatmeal
- ☐ Sprinkles
- ☐ Salt
- ☐ Pitcher of Water
- ☐ Spoon

Directions:

1. Pour a small amount of each pantry staple item (flour, sugar, rice, cornmeal, oatmeal, sprinkles, and salt) into its own bowl.

2. Invite your preschooler to test which items will dissolve (disappear) in water.

3. Ask him to pick one bowl to begin testing. Ask him if he thinks the item will dissolve.

4. Help him pour water from the pitcher into one bowl at a time.

5. He will then stir the mixture.

6. Ask him if his prediction was correct.

7. Continue Steps 3-6 for each bowl.

Appendix

If you need extra copies of the appendix pages,
please visit this link to download more appendix pages:

www.bestmomideas.com/ultimate-preschool-printouts

Password: bestmomideas9mx4

My name is

_____

My name has

[ ]

letters.

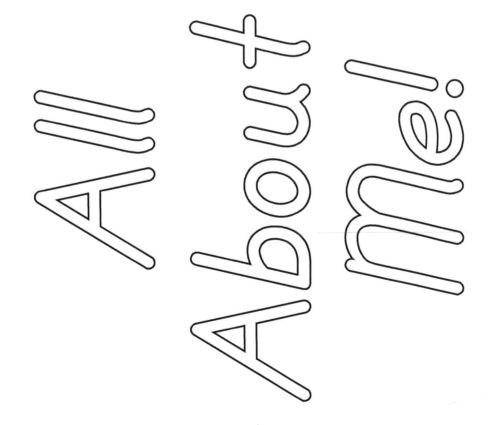

All About me!

I am

years old.

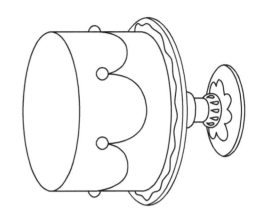

My Portrait

cut along line

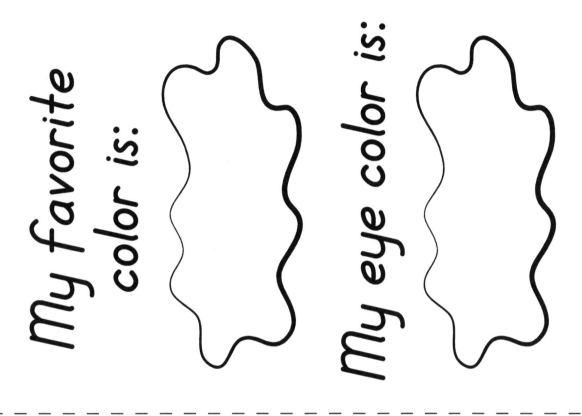

My favorite color is:

My eye color is:

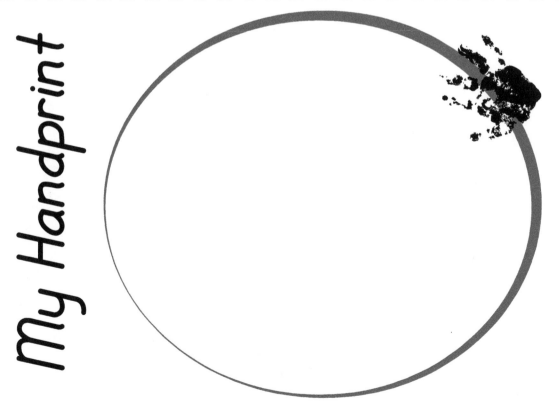

My Handprint

cut along line

When I grow up
I want to be a:

My hair color is:

My favorite
animal is:

Measurement							
Body Part	Head	Ear	Hand	Arm	Foot	Leg	Height

Measurement							
Body Part	Head	Ear	Hand	Arm	Foot	Leg	Height

cut along line

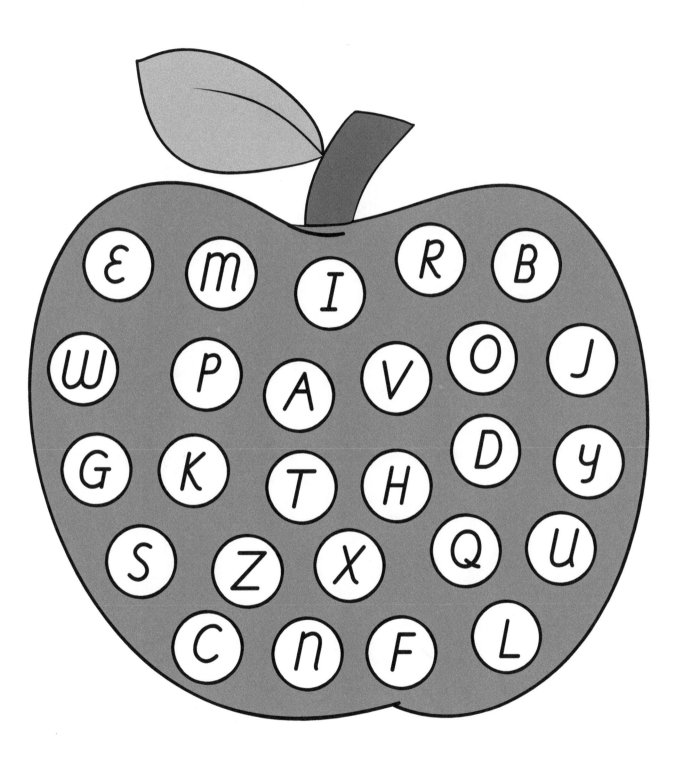

cut along line

Parts of an Apple

Color the parts of the apple. If you'd like, try to trace the labels.

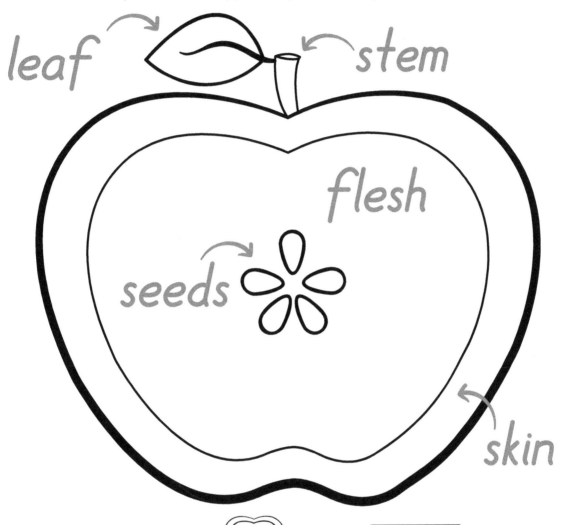

leaf · stem · flesh · seeds · skin

1. Color the  skin  .
2. Color the seeds  .
3. Color the leaf  .
4. Color the stem  .

cut along line

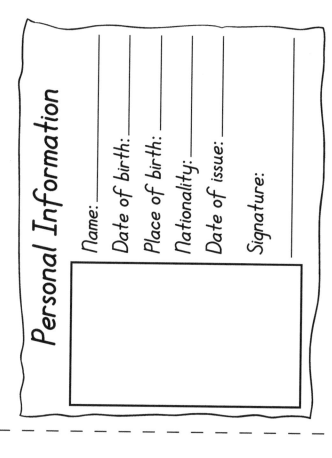

Personal Information

Name: _____

Date of birth: _____

Place of birth: _____

Nationality: _____

Date of issue: _____

Signature: _____

Color each continent as you learn about it.

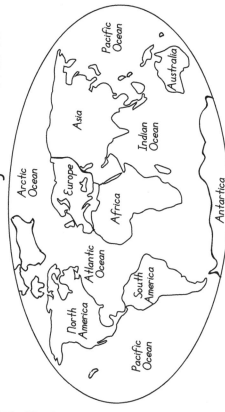

My Passport

cut along line

cut along line

Antarctica

Favorite Thing You Learned:

Africa

Favorite Thing You Learned:

Australia

Favorite Thing You Learned:

Asia

Favorite Thing You Learned:

North America

Favorite Thing You Learned:

Europe

Favorite Thing You Learned:

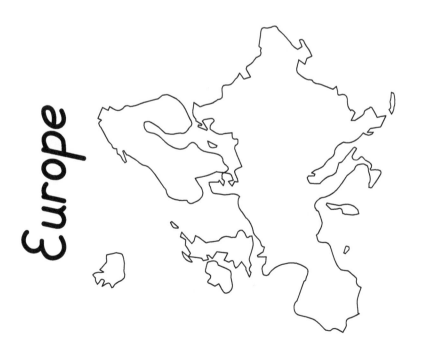

South America

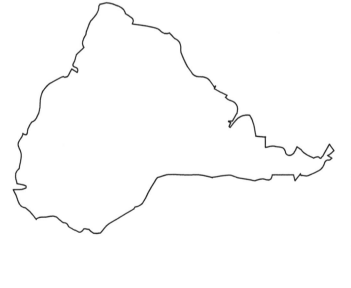

Favorite Thing You Learned:

cut along line

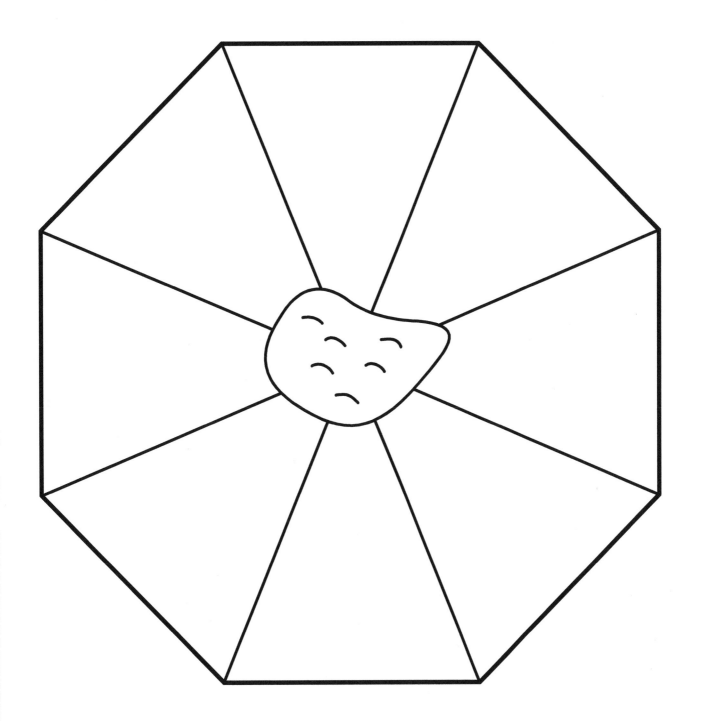

一	yī	1
二	èr	2
三	sān	3
四	sì	4
五	wū	5
六	liù	6
七	qī	7
八	bā	8
九	jiū	9
十	shí	10
大	dà	Big
小	xiāo	Small

How to use Chopsticks

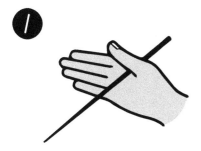

Place chopstick between
pointer finger and thumb.
Balance it on the ring finger.

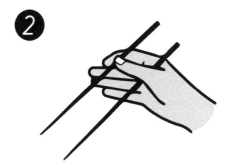

Place second chopstick between
pointer finger and thumb.
Rest it on your middle finger.

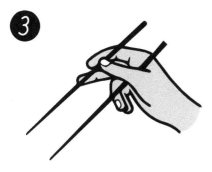

Use thumb, pointer and middle finger
to grasp the second chopstick
more tightly.

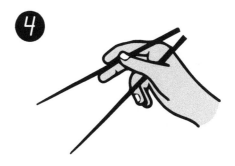

Index and middle fingers do
all lifting with the second chopstick.

Using index and middle fingers
close chopsticks over the food.

Well Done!

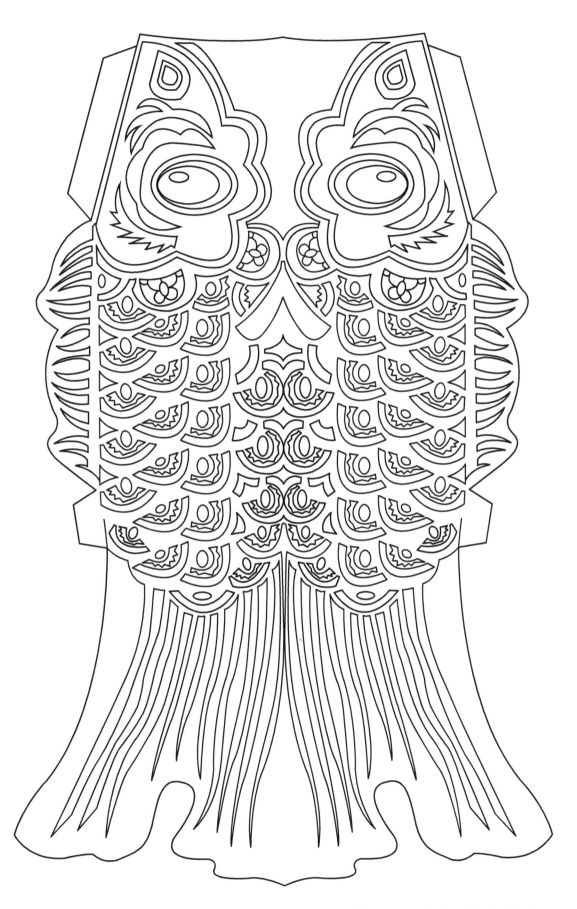

cut along line

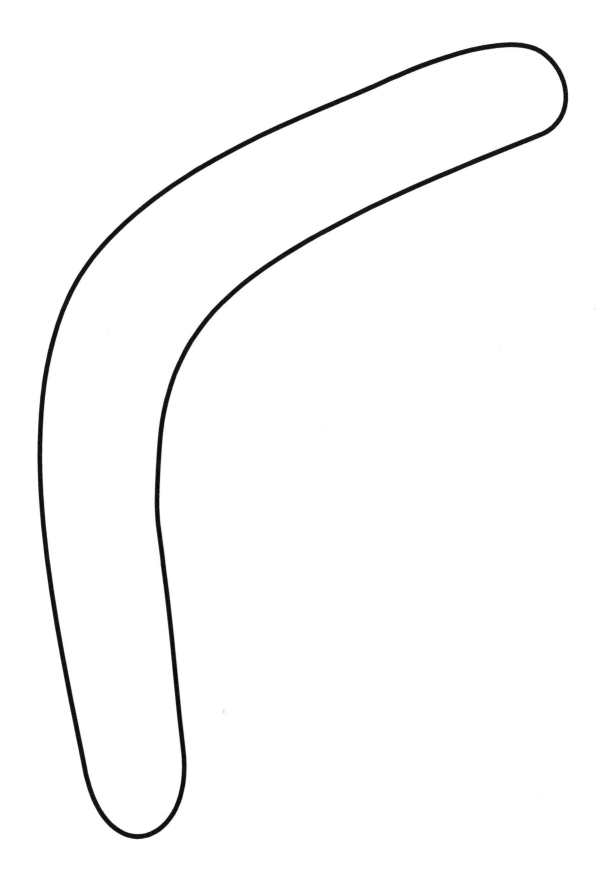

cut along line

Finished Craft

cut along line

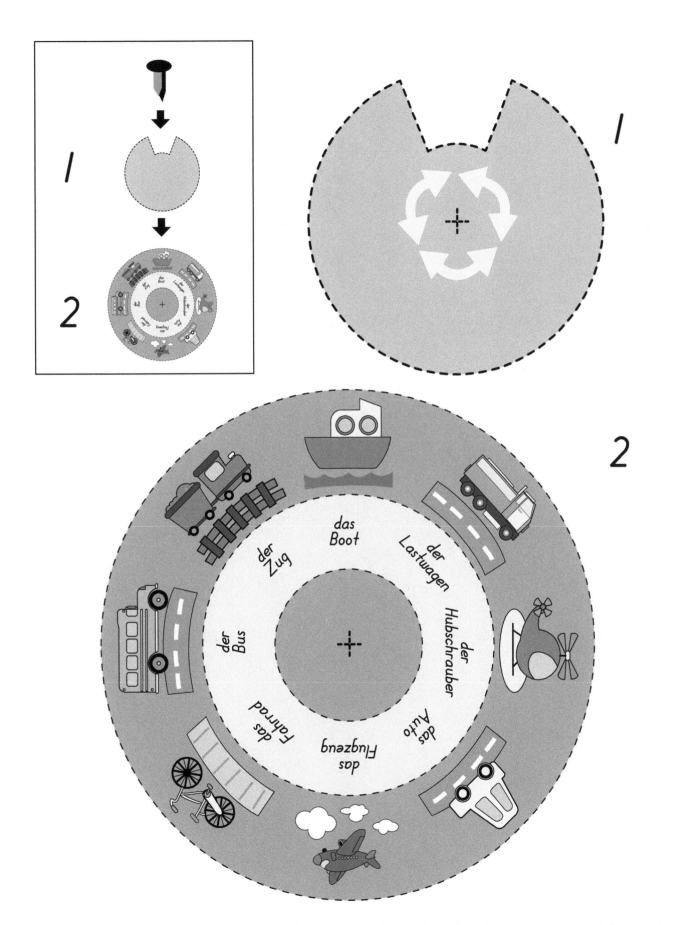

1

2

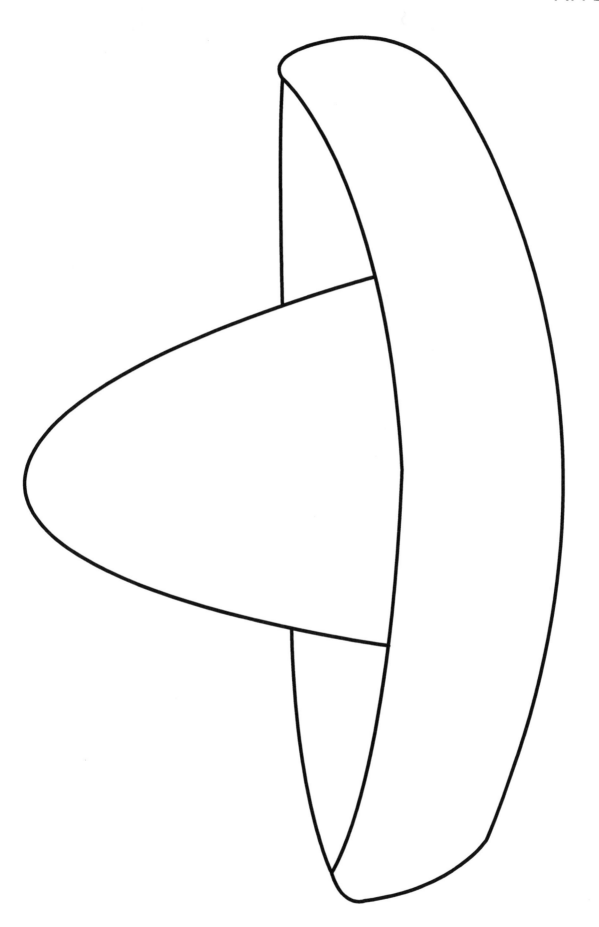

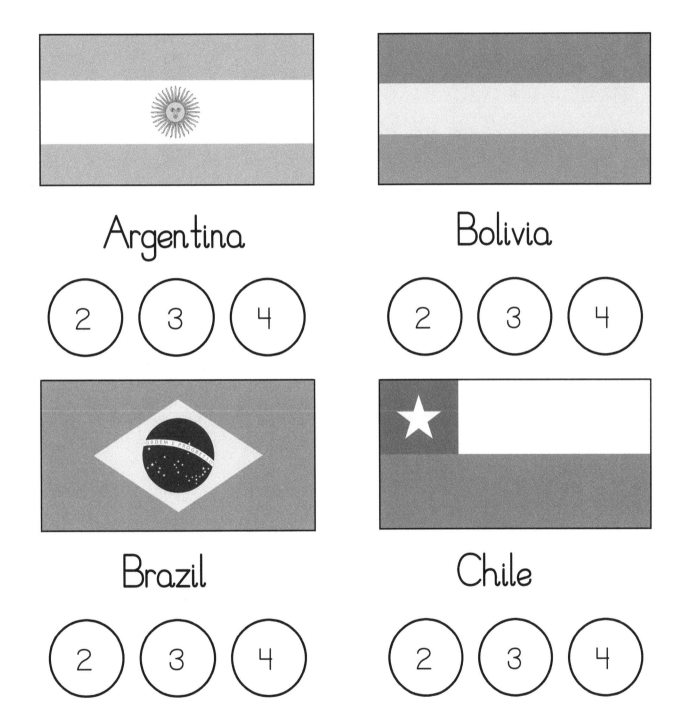

Argentina

2 3 4

Bolivia

2 3 4

Brazil

2 3 4

Chile

2 3 4

Paraguay

2   3   4

Peru

2   3   4

Suriname

2   3   4

Uruguay

2   3   4

Venezuela

2   3   4

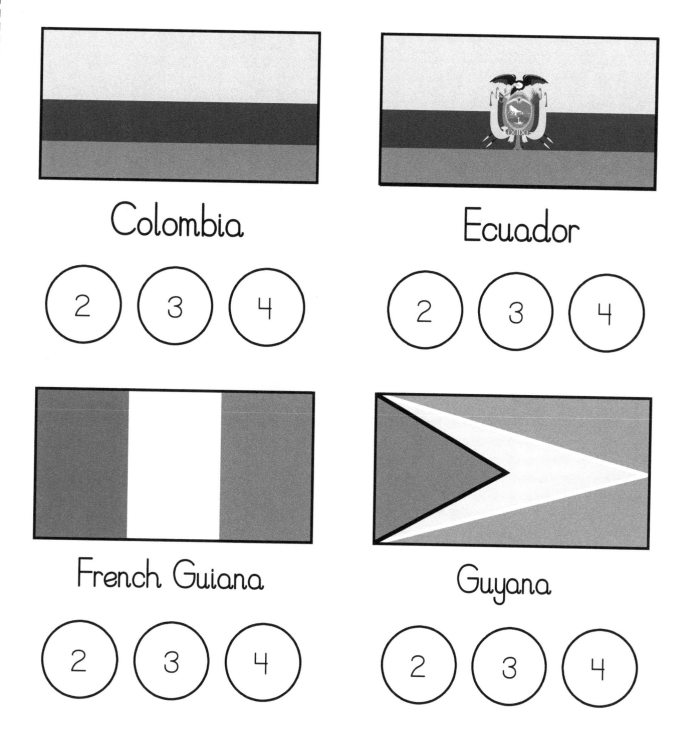

Colombia

2   3   4

Ecuador

2   3   4

French Guiana

2   3   4

Guyana

2   3   4

Living	Nonliving

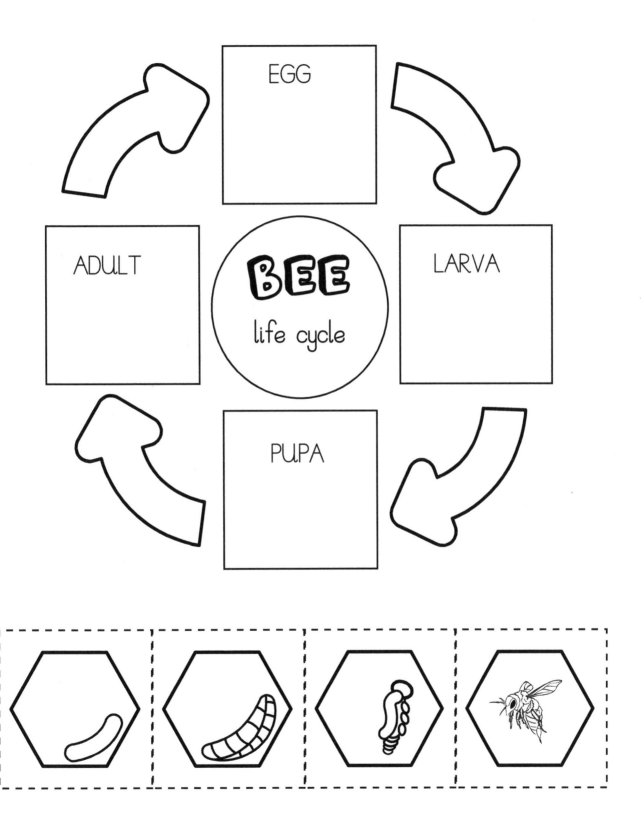

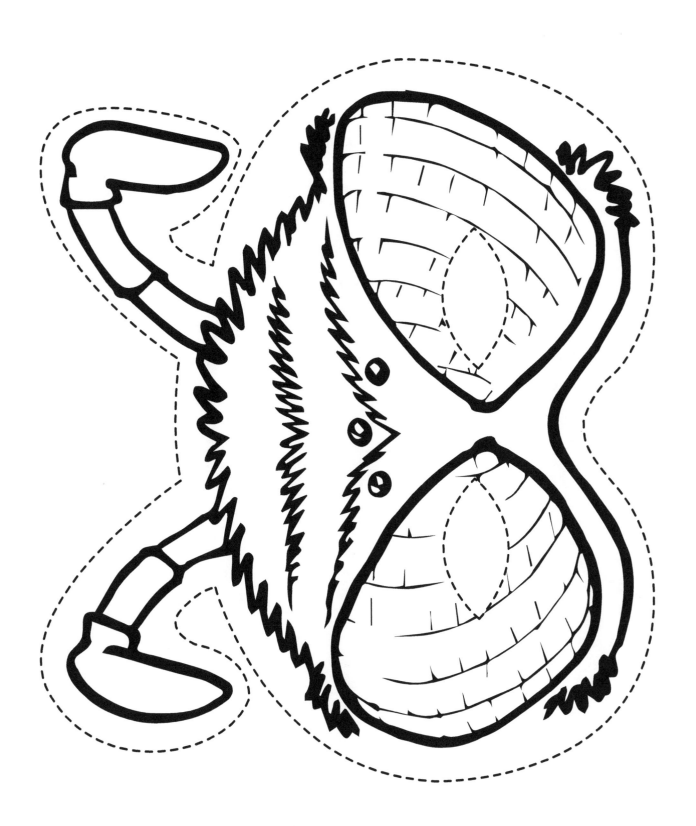

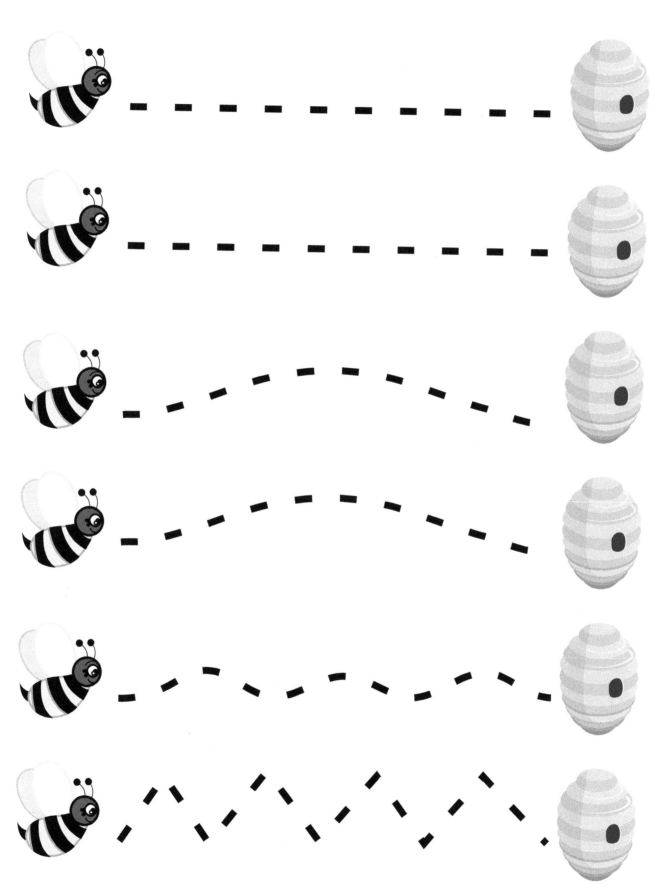

cut along line

Head | Eyes | Antennae | Thorax

Abdomen | Leg | Stinger

Wing | Wings

cut along line

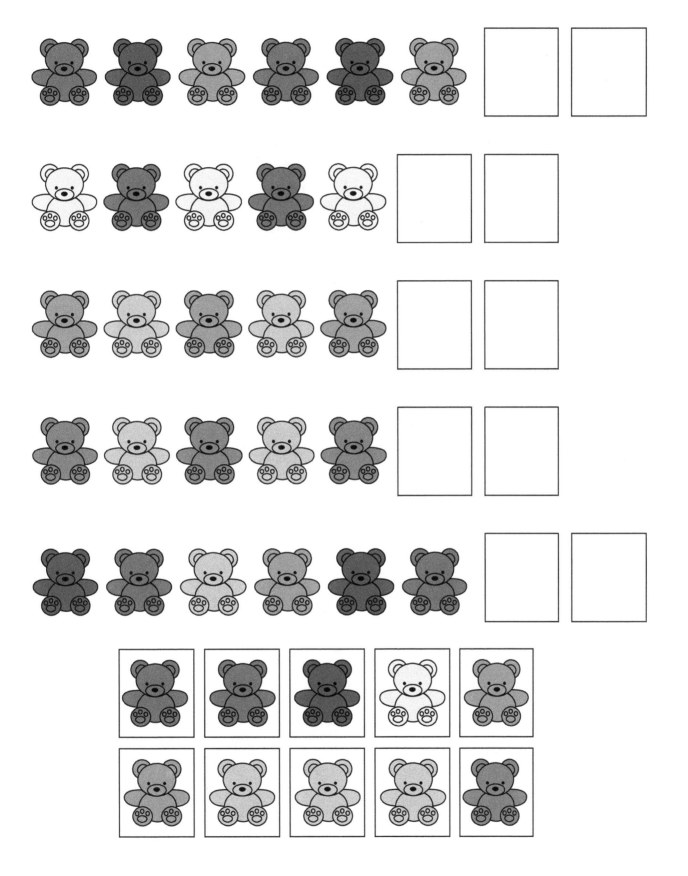

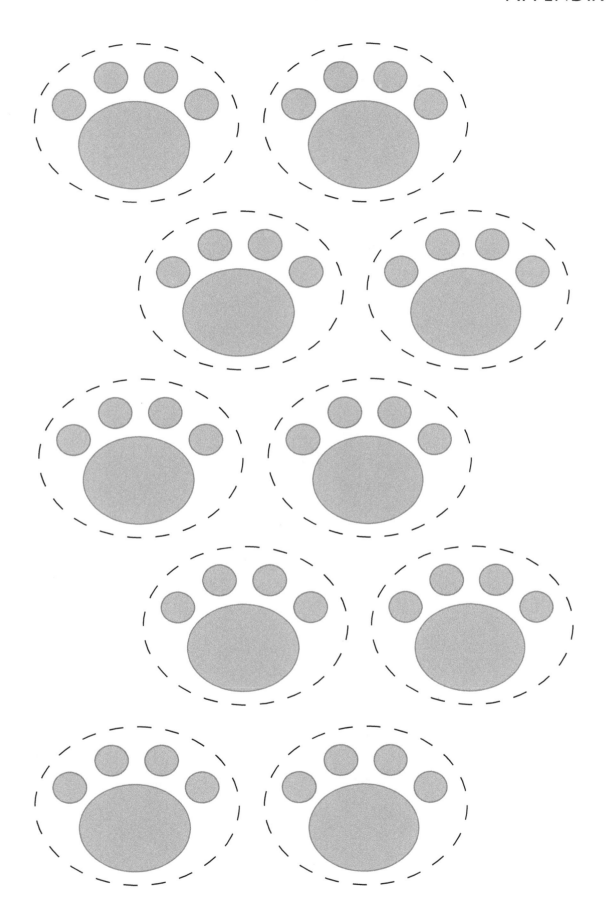

cut along line

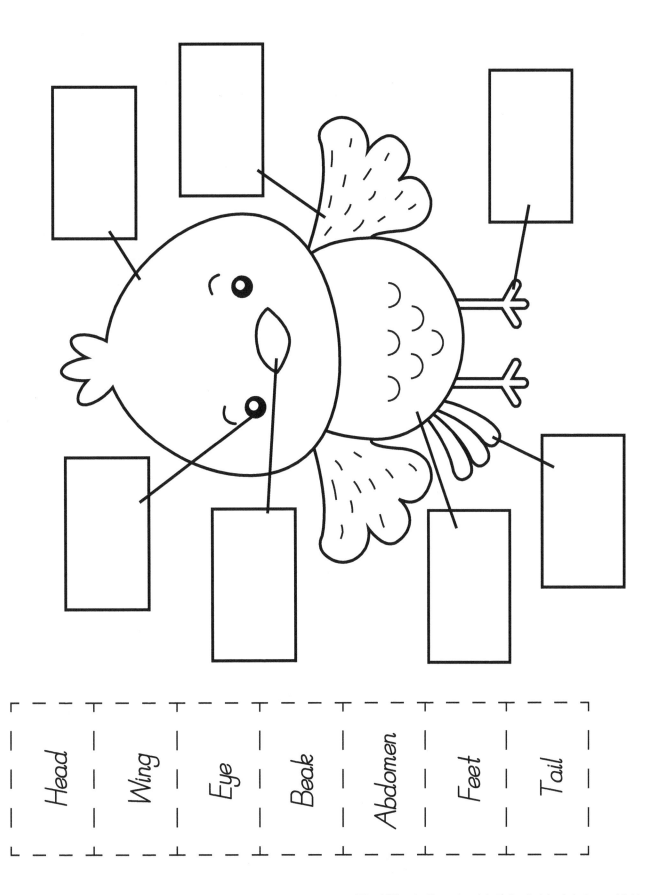

Head   Wing   Eye   Beak   Abdomen   Feet   Tail

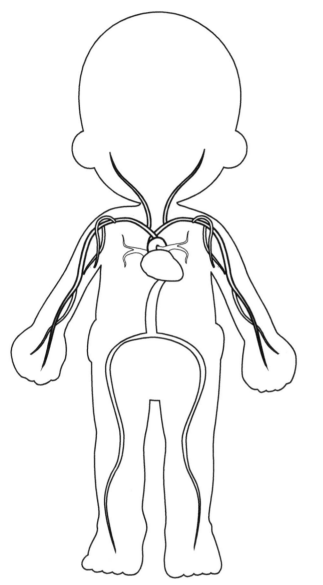

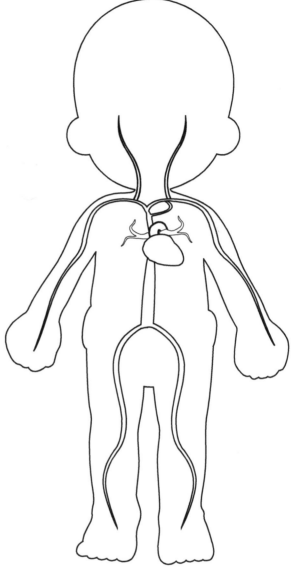

Arteries carry blood with

oxygen away from the heart

to all parts of the body.

Color the arteries red.

Veins bring blood back to the

heart from all the parts of

the body.

Color the veins blue.

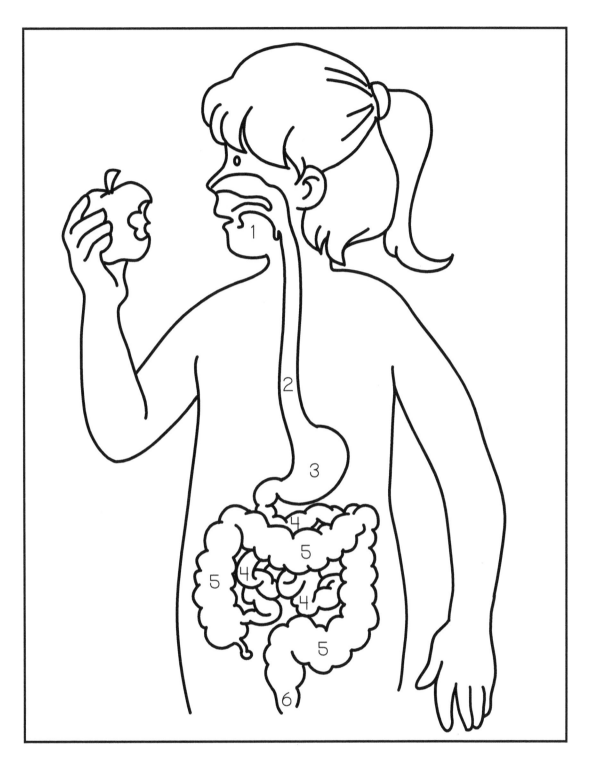

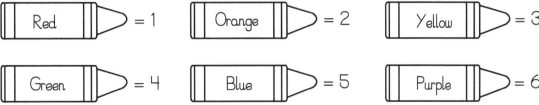

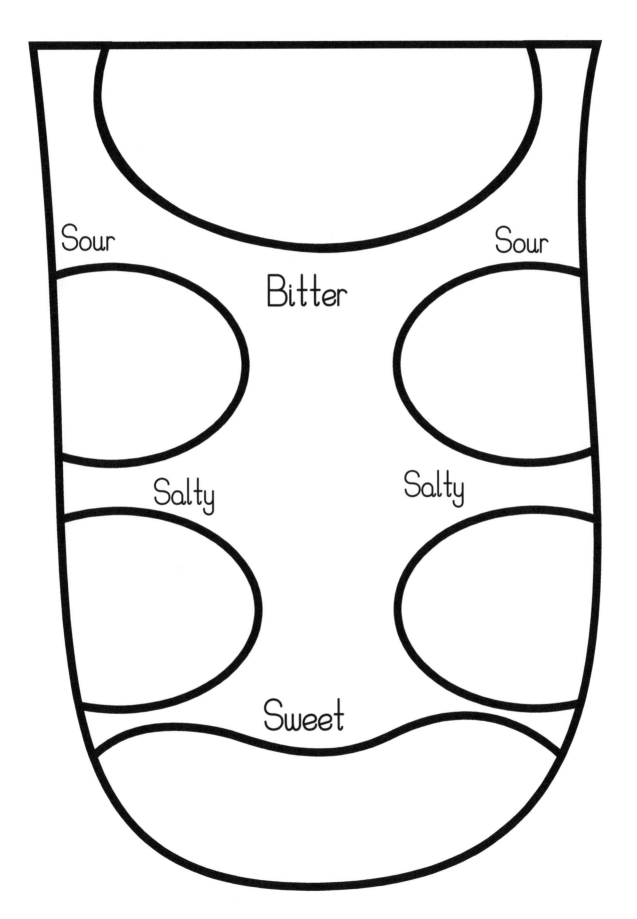

Sour Bitter Sour

Salty Salty

Sweet

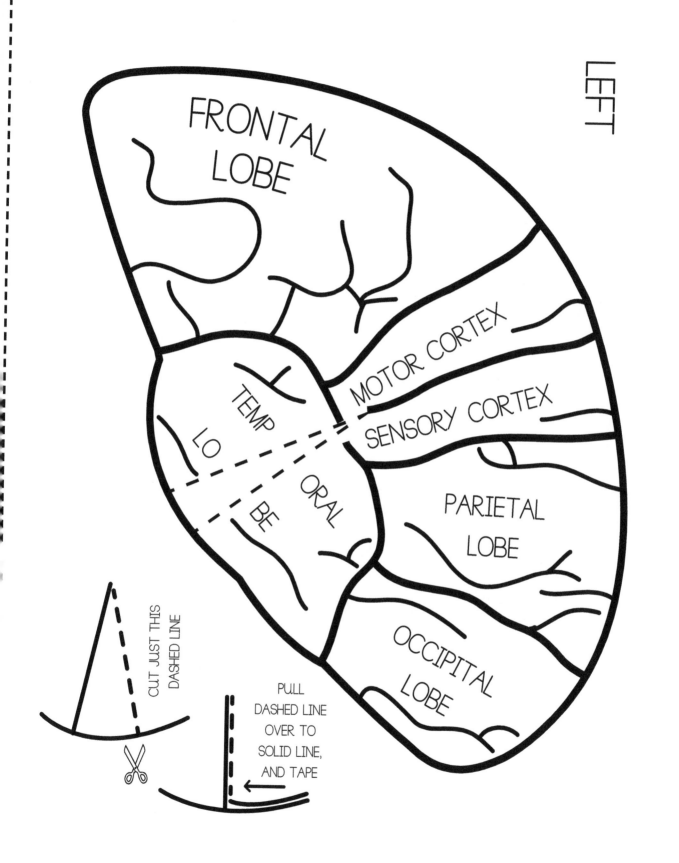

LEFT

FRONTAL LOBE

MOTOR CORTEX

SENSORY CORTEX

TEMP LO ORAL BE

PARIETAL LOBE

OCCIPITAL LOBE

CUT JUST THIS DASHED LINE

PULL DASHED LINE OVER TO SOLID LINE, AND TAPE

cut along line

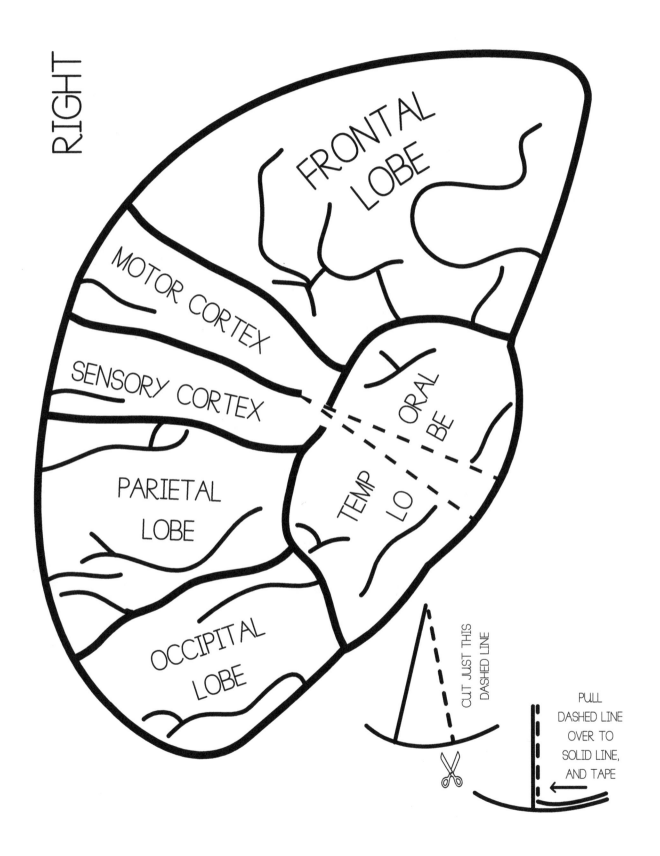

RIGHT

FRONTAL LOBE

MOTOR CORTEX

SENSORY CORTEX

TEMPORAL LOBE

PARIETAL LOBE

OCCIPITAL LOBE

CUT JUST THIS DASHED LINE

PULL DASHED LINE OVER TO SOLID LINE, AND TAPE

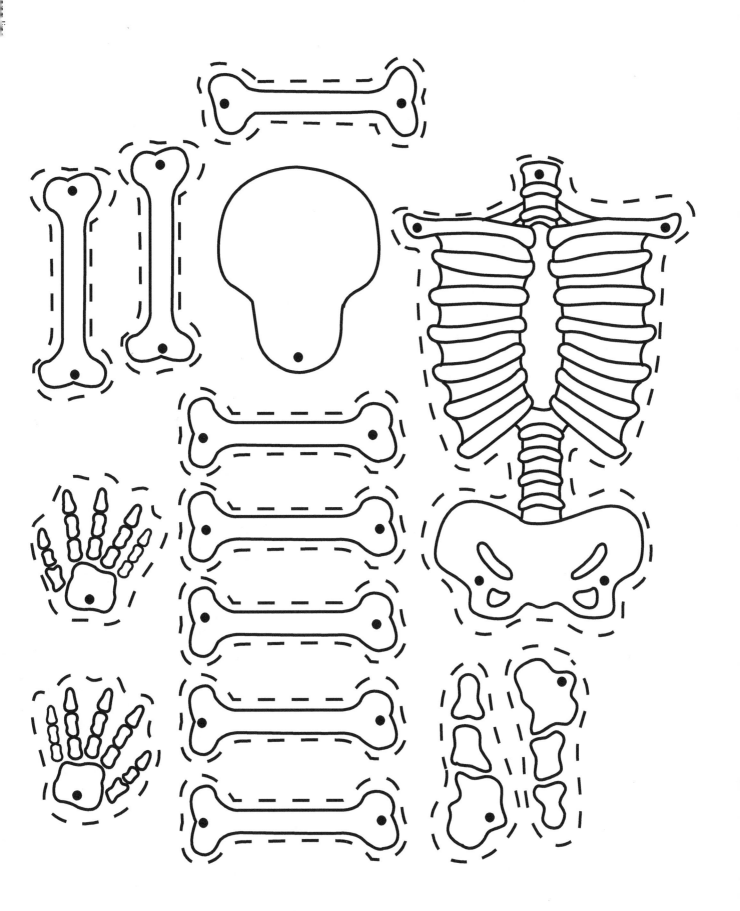

cut along line

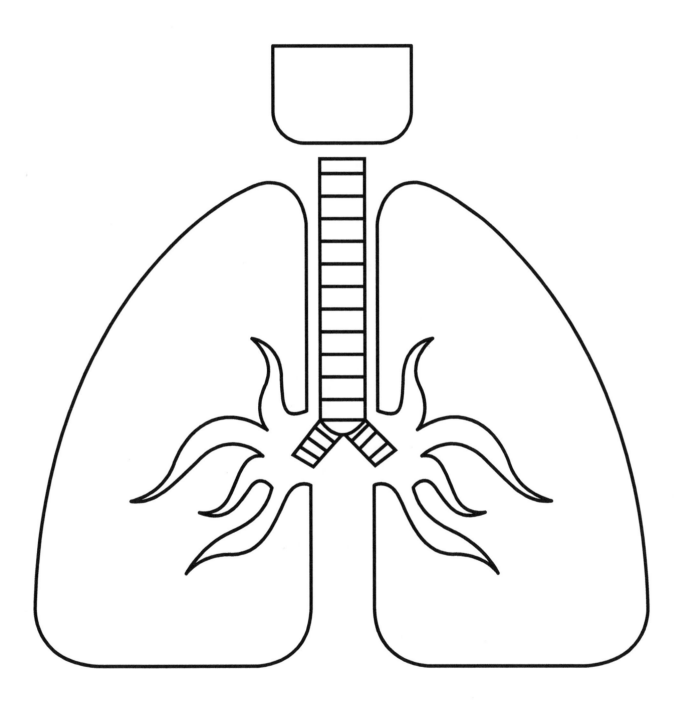

cut along line

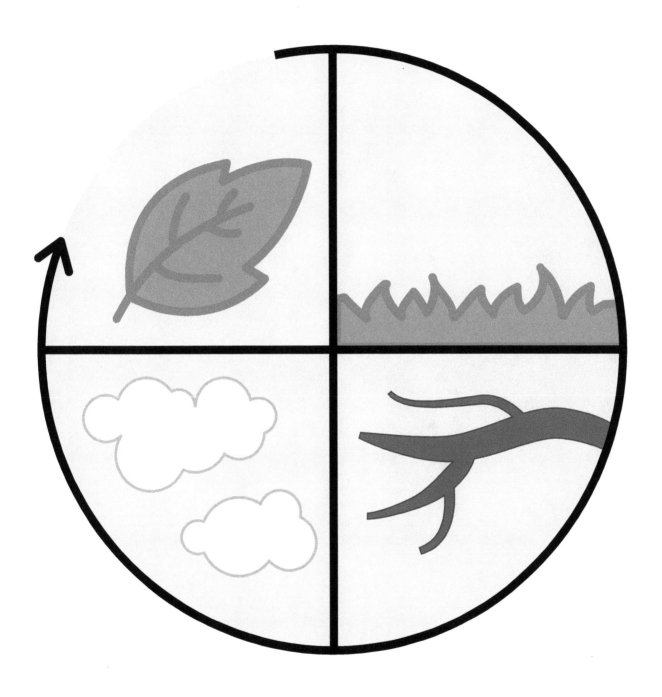

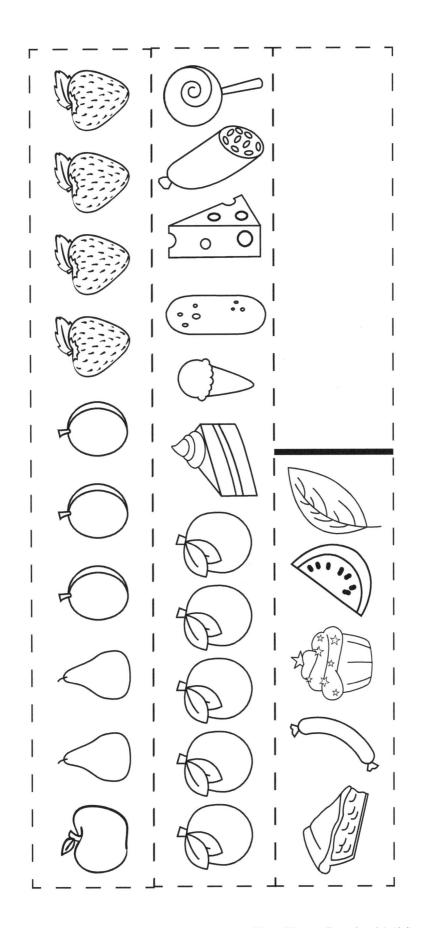

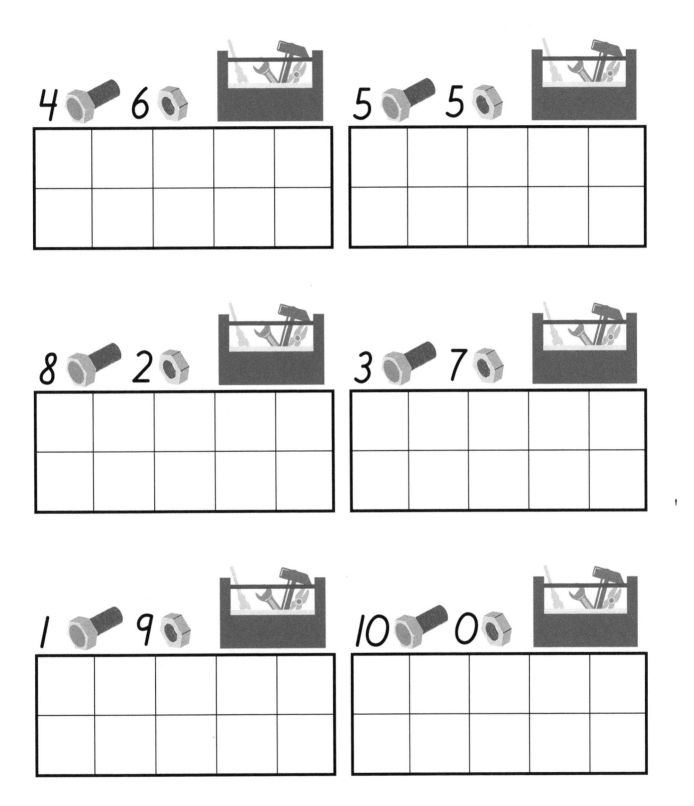

Hammer

Toolbox

Crane

Screwdriver

Bulldozer

Pliers

Cone

Excavator

Wrench

Tyrannosaurus Rex

Stegosaurus

Ankylosaurus

Brachiosaurus

Triceratops

Iguanodon

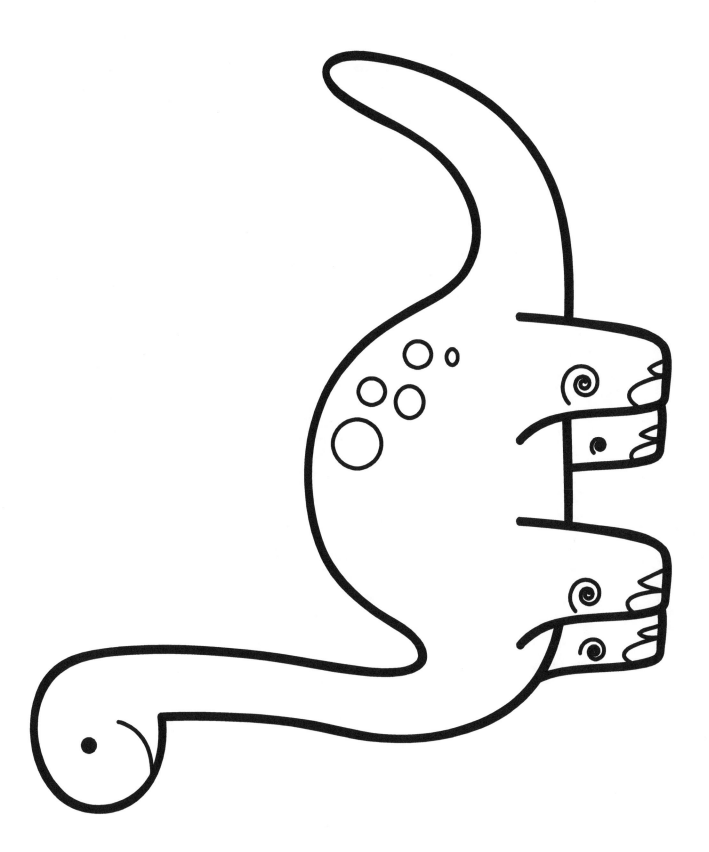

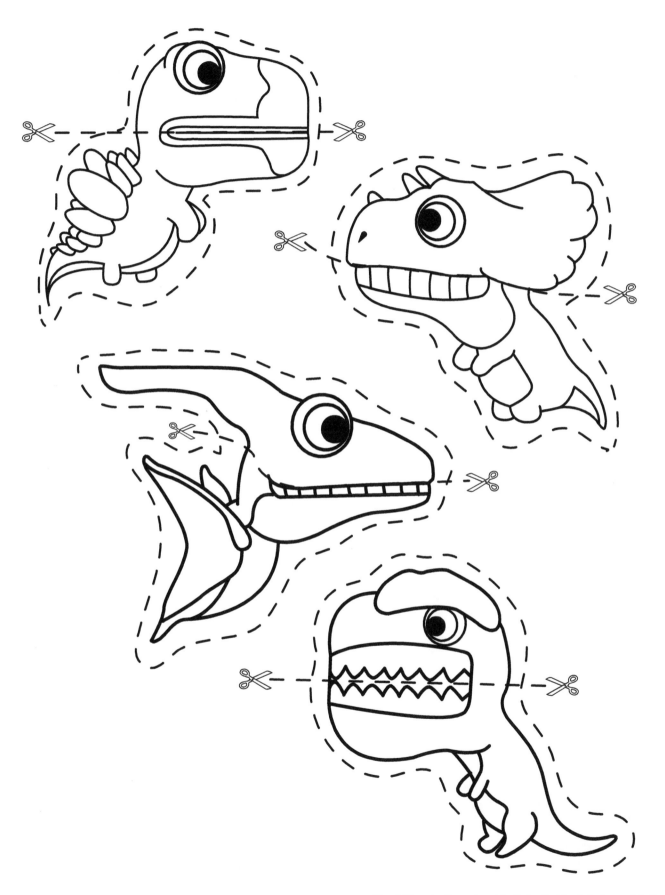

mom

DAD

SISTER

BROTHER

GRANDMA

GRANDPA

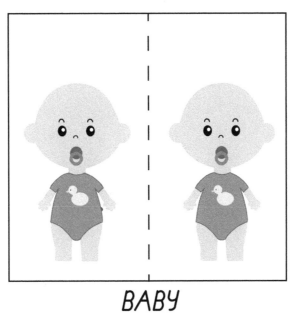

BABY

1- Your first clue is near where you eat. Go there now and look under your seat.

2- The whole family has one, but they never share. They're not made for hair. They're hard but soft on your teeth.

3- Getting this clue would be a joy. Look for it where you would put your toy.

4- If you want to find more clues, look in the place where you put your shoes.

5- You are finding clues and feeling bold, now go to the place that keeps food really cold.

6- While you are up walking around, go to the place where you go to lay down.

7- Rose are red, Violets are blue, find the next clue where you shampoo.

8- Yay! You did it!

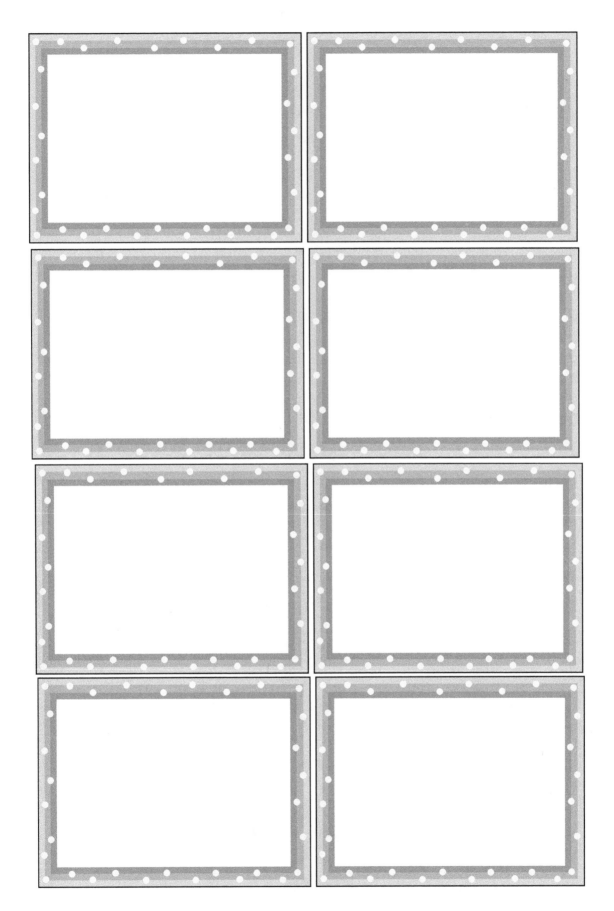

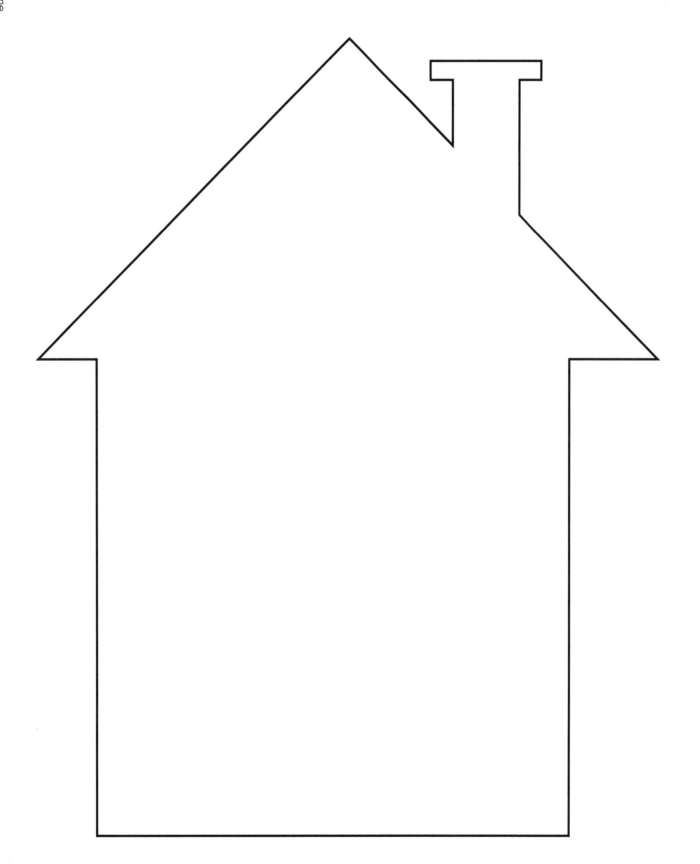

cut along line

BEING A FRIEND	NOT BEING A FRIEND

cut along line

Hands are not for hitting!

Hands are for...

    Waving + Washing

    Clapping + Counting

    Drawing + Doodling

    Holding + Hugging

Hands are NOT for hitting!

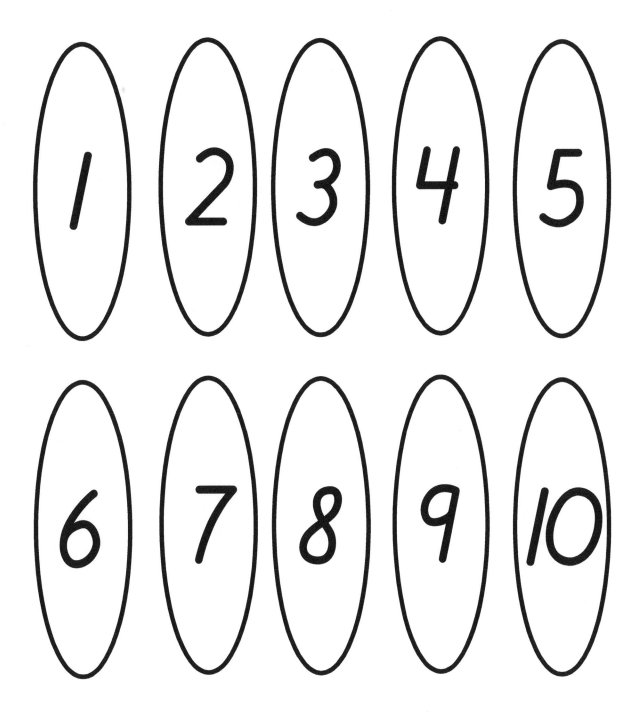

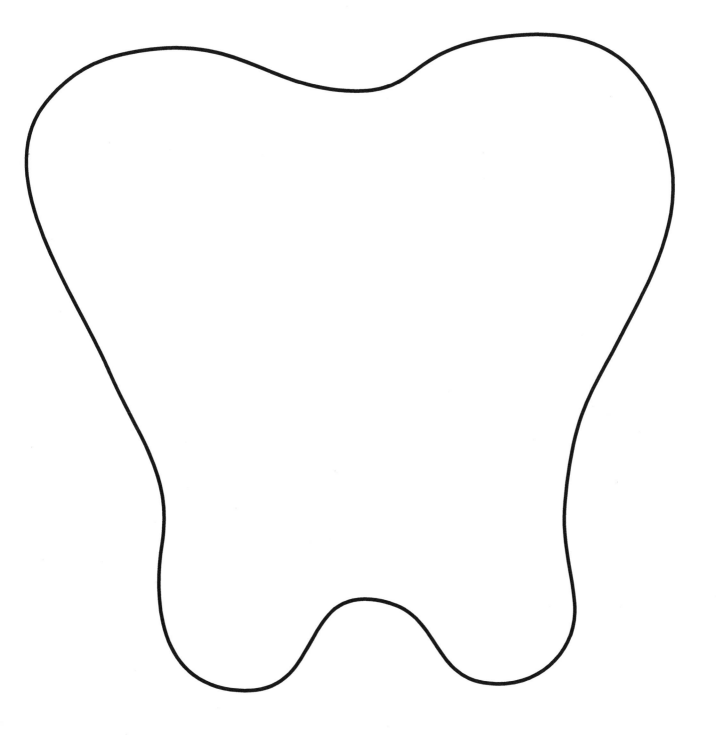

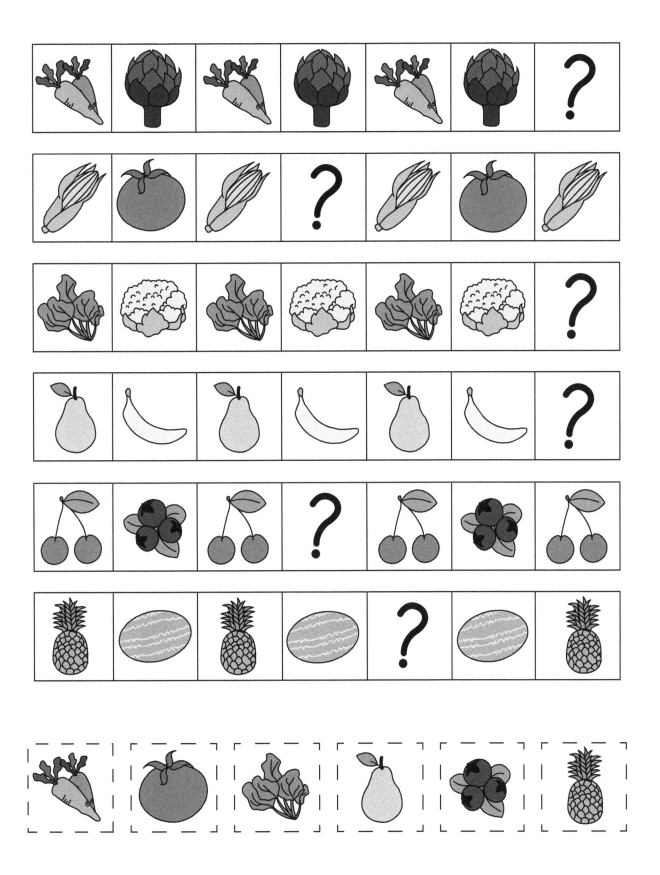

OUTSIDE	INSIDE

cut along line

I have 5 pennies.	I have 2 quarters.
I have 3 dimes.	I have 2 dimes.
I have 4 nickels.	I have 1 penny.
I have 6 nickels.	I have 3 quarters.

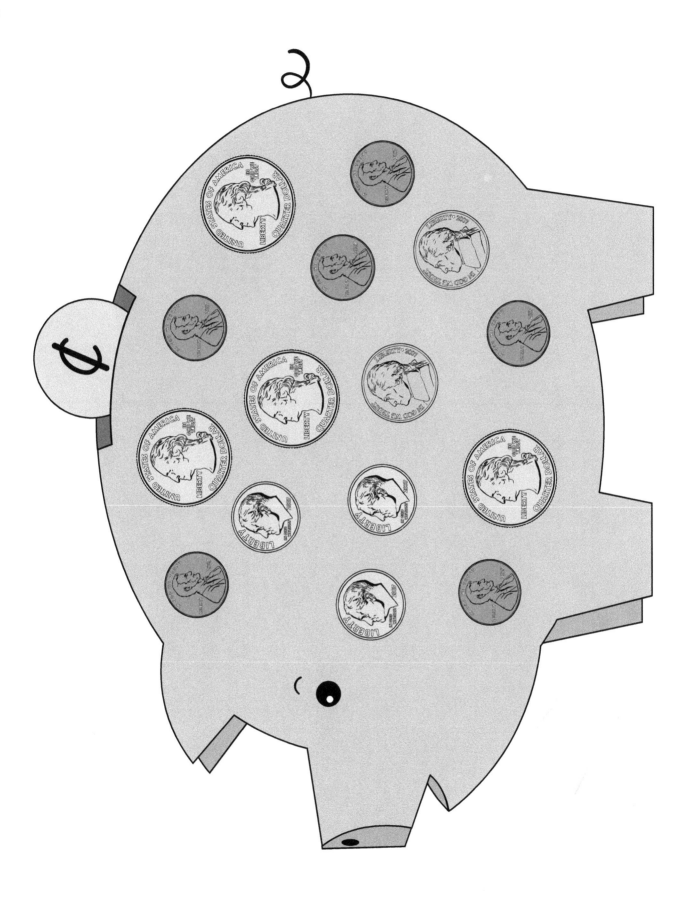

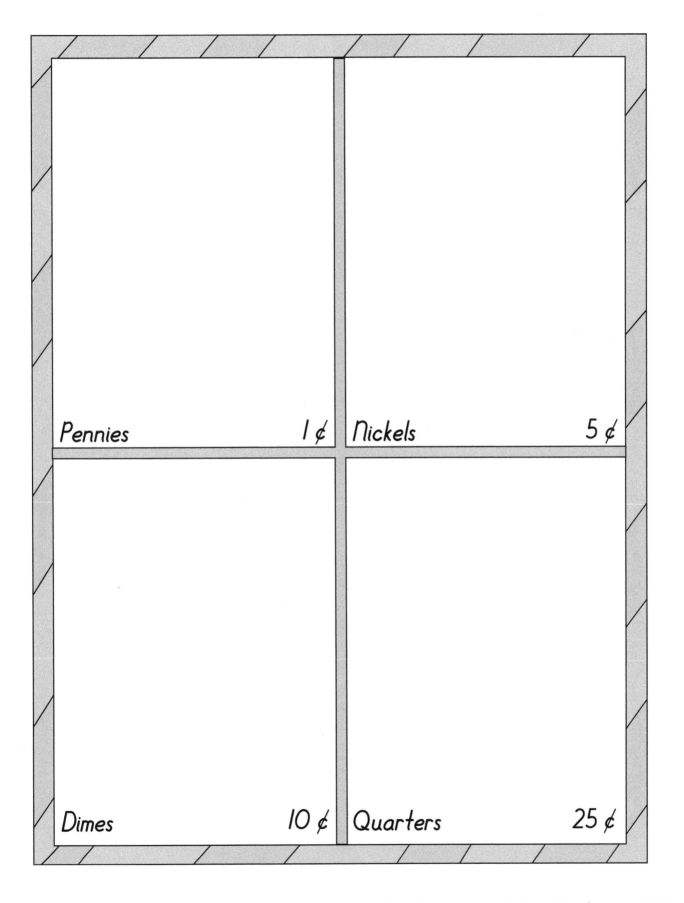

Pennies   1 ¢

Nickels   5 ¢

Dimes   10 ¢

Quarters   25 ¢

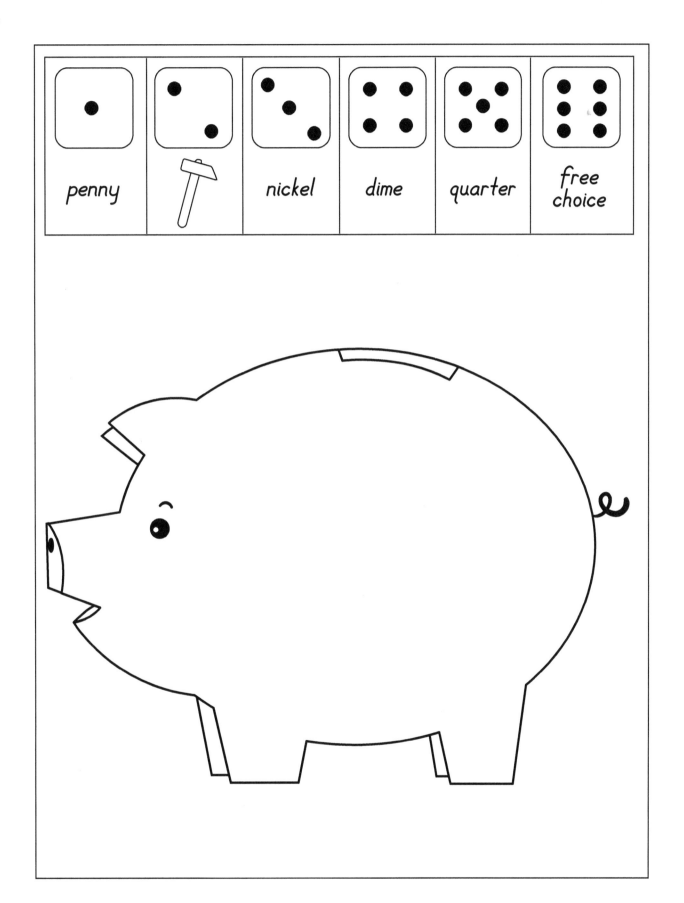

| penny | | nickel | dime | quarter | free choice |

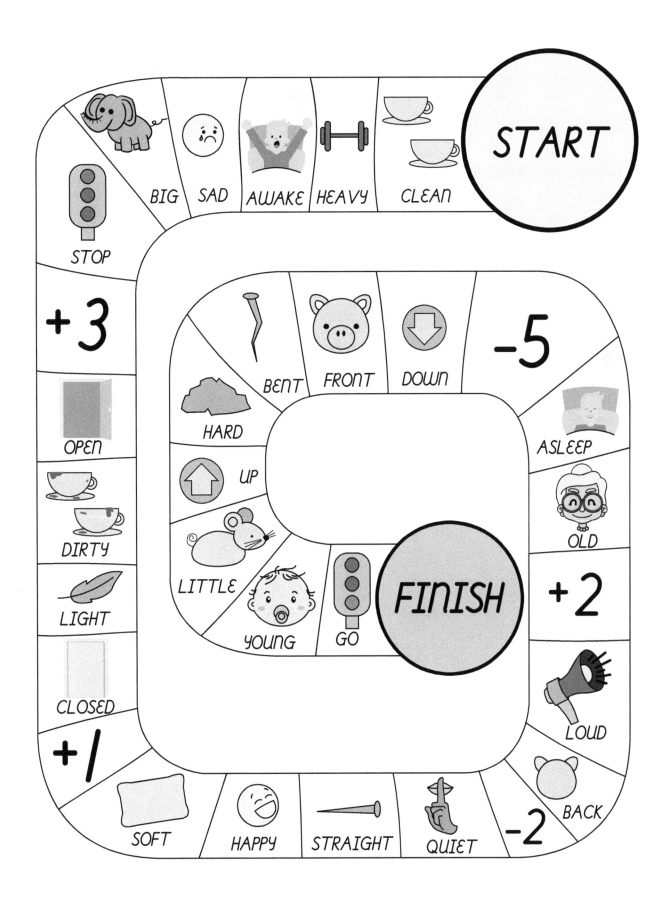

DAY

UP

ASLEEP

BIG

BOY

HOT

 AWAKE

 GIRL

 SMALL

 NIGHT

 COLD

 DOWN

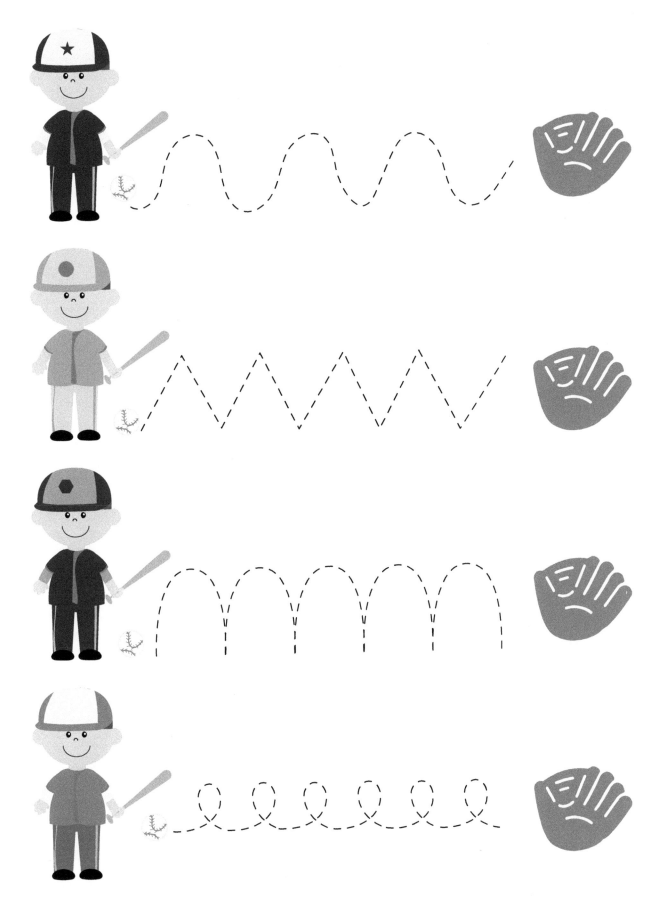

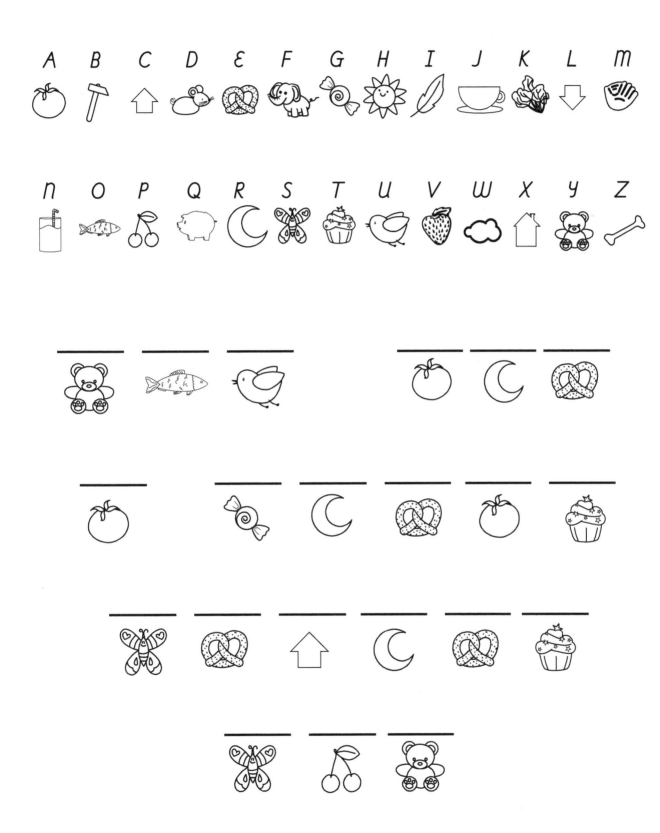

Thank you for welcoming me into your home!
I hope you and your child liked learning together with this book!

If you enjoyed this book, it would mean so much to me
if you wrote a review so other moms can learn from your experience.

-♡- Autumn

Autumn@BestMomIdeas.com

Discover Autumn's Other Books

Early Learning Series

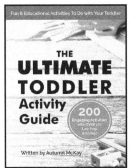

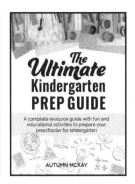

Early Learning Workbook Series

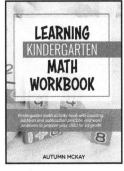
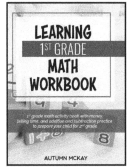

www.BestMomIdeas.com   @BestMomIdeas   Best Mom Ideas

CPSIA information can be obtained
at www.ICGtesting.com
Printed in the USA
BVHW012018090421
604337BV00032B/1997